THE
APRIL
GAME

By
DIOGENES

THE APRIL GAME
Secrets of an Internal Revenue Agent

PꝐP

A PLAYBOY PRESS BOOK

Published simultaneously in the United States and Canada by Playboy Press, Chicago, Illinois. Printed in the United States of America. Library of Congress Catalog Card Number: 72-96886. First edition.

PLAYBOY and Rabbit Head design are trademarks of Playboy, 919 North Michigan Avenue, Chicago, Illinois 60611 (U.S.A.), Reg. U.S. Pat. Off., marca registrada, marque déposée.

CONTENTS

PART III YOU AND ME AGAINST THE TAX

PART I

THE PEOPLE VERSUS THE TAX

*Wherein we reflect upon a tax
that nobody likes, nobody
ever has liked and nobody
ever will like.
And wherein we consider the
two Dicta of Diogenes.
The First Dictum being:
The more heavily a man is
supposed to be taxed, the
more power he has to escape
being taxed.
The Second Dictum being:
If a taxpayer thinks he can
cheat safely, he probably will.*

Chapter 1

THE
GAME

My group chief was feeling morose and vindictive one morning. "Enough jokes!" he bellowed. He waved a 1040 at me. It was a mottled reddish-brown. The taxpayer had splashed it with blood. "Get ahold of this silly bastard," the chief roared, "and audit the hell out of him! If he's got any more blood in him, squeeze it to the last drop!"

I went to see the taxpayer. He was a small, mild fellow in the fabric-importing business. He was apologetic. He assured me the blood was only beef blood. "I don't often do dumb things like that," he said, "but I was at the end of my rope last April. With costs and taxes rising the way they are, Jeez . . ."

"Okay, okay," I said, "forget it. Let's get down to business."

We did. As it turned out, there wasn't much extra

blood to be squeezed. The worst I could do was disallow some claimed pilferage losses that the taxpayer couldn't substantiate. The tax deficiency and interest came to about 30 bucks.

"Cheer up," I said. "It isn't blood. It's only money."

He nodded and said he guessed I was right. While I was packing my briefcase he went into another room to talk to his wife. A minute later he came back and asked if I'd care to have a drink with them.

It was the end of a long day. I said sure. I was happy to think the taxpayer harbored no residue of ill will and I wanted him to know I harbored none either. I figured a companionable drink would be good for IRS-taxpayer relations. Though the task is patently impossible, we at IRS are always trying to make taxpayers love us.

But this particular TP couldn't resist stating his protest one last time. His wife came in wearing a grin and carrying a tray of drinks. They were Bloody Marys.

Revenue agents and taxpayers are natural adversaries. We may be polite to each other and may even smile like good sports, but we will never be friends.

Conversely, we need not be enemies. I hope to convince you before the end of this book that I am not your enemy, especially if you are a middle-income taxpayer. I like middle-income TPs (am one myself, as a matter of fact) and have long felt that the present tax setup in this country puts a distinctly unfair burden on this class of citizens. I've been preaching for years around the Revenue Service that the TPs in the middle need a break, and sometimes I've given them private, unofficial breaks in the course of auditing them.

No, I am not your enemy. I am only your adversary.

The difference is worth noting. I will never get mad at you for trying to win the game. I won't even get mad at you for getting mad at me. I know it is more than a game to you.

Another taxpayer mailed us a turnip, along with a note saying we were welcome to any blood we could get out of it. Somebody cut a slice out of the turnip and mailed the slice back, folded inside a letter. The letter said, "Enclosed please find refund. Affectionately, U.S. Treasury."

Other taxpayers signal their protests by sending us old shirts (off their backs) and tea bags (to remind us of the Boston Tea Party). We get a lot of returns dropped into mailboxes without stamps. The taxpayers explain grumpily that they are down to their last eight cents. We get bills from TPs demanding that we pay for aspirin, ulcer medication and tranquilizers. One fellow sent us a bag of hair that he claimed to have torn from his scalp. Another paid his tax by mailing a few pounds of pennies, explaining that he had had to rob his youngster's piggy bank to satisfy us.

They love to needle us. We get a lot of returns each year from fictitious TPs. Some of them like to pretend they are millionaires. They send us bundles of play money or fake checks in huge amounts. Others claim poverty. One fictitious taxpayer named Poor Richard said his taxable income was one cent. Cellophane-taped to his return was his tax payment—a pie-slice segment hacksawed out of a penny.

Catherine III Meda Trinity Victoria Alix Nikolaivna Romanov is another nontaxpayer, probably fictitious, who dutifully files a return every year but sends no money. She claims to be a Russian princess and says that under a secret law that only she knows about she isn't required to pay taxes. Agents have tried to find who she really is but have never been able to track her down.

Still another non-TP filed his return with an apologetic letter saying he hadn't been able to figure out how much he owed. "If you will tell me what my tax liability is," he wrote, "I will humbly pay." On his return he gave his name as Jehovah and his occupation as God.

But most taxpayers play the game on a more pragmatic level. Their object is not only to one-up me but also to walk away with some hard-cash winnings. The Revenue Service never, never acknowledges this in its official statements, but it is generally assumed among agents that the majority of taxpayers cheat. Cheating is the part of the game that generates the greatest fun—not only for the millions of taxpayers who win the game each year, but also for agents like me. It is our job, and our delight, to match wits with the larcenous and the clever.

Like players in any other game, revenue agents enjoy reminiscing about adversaries they have met and beaten—and also those they couldn't beat. You will meet many of my own favorite adversaries in this book, and there are scores of others I could tell you about if we had a year or more of time. I don't know why some of them stand out more starkly in my memory than others. Perhaps some impressed me because they were more nimble or brazen than the average. Others, by contrast, were memorably dumb or naïve. Still others appear to have lodged in my memory because—well, because I grew fond of them, I suppose.

Charitable Charles, as I have taken the liberty of naming him, claimed to have given something like $7,000 worth of paintings to a university. Since this sum was nearly a quarter of his annual income, it caused a computer to hiccup and resulted in my being dispatched to audit the man.

The paintings, Charles explained, had been given to him over the years by his grandmother, now dead. There were about 70 of them, and he valued them at $100 apiece.

I asked, "How did you arrive at that value?"

He answered eagerly, as though he had been waiting years for the question to be asked. "An art dealer appraised them for me," he said. "And not only that, but the dealer actually sold a few for a hundred bucks each. So his appraisal has got to be realistic, right?"

I asked if he had any of the paintings left to show me. He had a couple. They looked dreadful. One was a seascape in which the sea looked something like blue corrugated cardboard. Another depicted a cat with a rather nightmarish, walleyed look. Since I know considerably less about art than about money, and since I didn't want to insult the taxpayer's dear old grandmother, I mumbled a polite comment and went away.

I phoned the university that had received the munificent gift. The art curator of the university library told me he had stored the paintings in the basement, where, he hoped, the light of day would never reach them.

"They have no value?" I asked.

"Well," he said, "the paint is nice and thick. They might have value as roof shingles."

I went around to see the art dealer. He said, "The curator doesn't know what he's talking about. I don't care what he says. I say the old lady's paintings are fine examples of folk art."

I examined his books. They showed he had sold three

of the paintings for $100 each, and he had declared that $300 as part of his gross income for the year. He remarked that he still had four of the paintings left and had high hopes of selling them for a similar price.

I was out of my depth. I went back to my office and appealed to higher authority. A woman special agent, knowledgeable about art, was assigned to the case. I asked her to go to the art shop and look at the paintings.

She posed as a customer. "How much do you want for this one?" she asked the dealer, holding up one of the old lady's landscapes.

"Ah—ten bucks," said the dealer.

"You've got to be kidding," she said.

They haggled their way down to two dollars, and then she pulled out her IRS credentials. The dealer took it coolly. He pointed out that art means different things to different people. "There are no set prices for works of art," he said. "If you think this painting is only worth two bucks, all right. I was willing to let you have it because I want to get rid of some old stock. But to somebody else the painting may be worth a hundred."

The agent asked, "Who was the customer who paid a hundred?"

The dealer shrugged. "A guy off the street. Never saw him before or since."

The woman agent was almost sure—as I was—that the mysterious customer was Charitable Charles himself, carefully setting up a tax gimmick. Either that, or Charitable Charles paid the dealer to fake the $100-apiece sales. But there was no easy way to prove it, and in the end we decided we didn't have a fraud case that would stand up. We simply disallowed most of Charitable Charles's deduction. We allowed $140—two bucks per painting. He didn't contest the decision, but shortly afterward he mailed me the painting of the walleyed cat, along with a somewhat bitter note saying he hoped his grandmother's ghost would haunt me. I gave the painting to a church bazaar in which my wife was involved.

Somebody bought it for $25.

I thought about that for a long time when I was making out my own tax return. I started by taking a charitable deduction of $25. Then I crossed that out and made it two dollars. Finally I crossed out the two dollars and decided to forget the whole crazy episode.

Yet it still nags me. Was Charles a cheat? Did he conspire with the art dealer? Or were they both telling the truth? Sometimes, questions like these cannot be answered.

Joe the Detective aroused my suspicions from the beginning. He had a small private-eye outfit that earned its living mainly by working for industrial companies, checking the backgrounds of employees who were being considered for important or sensitive jobs. His tax return said his gross income from clients' fees was about $40,000. However, he claimed to have paid about $30,000 to freelance operatives who worked on various cases for him. With office rent, travel and other expenses also deducted, his net business income came to about $5,000.

It didn't look right to me. Why would a man spend three-fourths of his gross receipts hiring other people to work for him? Why wouldn't he do more of the work himself?

Joe the Detective was a small, dark-haired man with an uncanny resemblance to Humphrey Bogart. When I questioned him about his free-lance operatives, he shrugged and said that was the nature of the business. "Some years I make more money than other years," he said. "This was a bad year. What else can I tell you?"

"But why do you have to hire all these people?"

"Because I always have several investigations going on at once. I'll need a guy checking job records in one place and another guy asking questions someplace else. I'd do it all myself if I could, but I can only be in one place at a time."

I still didn't like it. I asked him for canceled checks to substantiate the claimed payments to operatives. He came up with them instantly. They were neatly stacked and bundled. They showed payments to eight different people, of whom three were women. Each had evidently earned about $4,000 during the year.

I made a list of the eight names and asked Joe for their addresses and phone numbers. He didn't like that and asked my reasons. I mumbled something about spot-checking to see whether the operatives had declared their incomes honestly. He frowned and looked uncomfortable. "I don't like my operatives' identities to be known to a lot of people," he said.

I pointed out that he had already been required to reveal their identities to IRS. He had been required to file 1099 information forms on them, showing their addresses, Social Security numbers and the amount paid to each. "You *did* file 1099s, didn't you?" I asked sternly.

"Of course," he said promptly. He was tax-wise enough to know that I could track down the operatives through the 1099s if I wanted the information badly enough. He could gain nothing by refusing to give me the addresses and phone numbers. In fact he could get into serious trouble. A refusal to give relevant data to a revenue agent can lead to a presumption of willful fraud.

I went away with my list of operatives. Back at my office I picked the first one on the list, a Mrs. Adams, and phoned her. I identified myself and said I was interested in the nature of the work she performed for Joe the Detective.

As she was giving her answer, I had the distinct impression that she had been coached. She spoke almost as though she was reciting a memorized explanation. "My work is mainly—um—verification of job applicants' statements," she said. "If an applicant claims to have held a certain position with a certain company . . ."

Another odd fact about Mrs. Adams was that her voice had a reedy, tremulous quality, as though she might be very old. The more I probed into this situation, the less I liked it.

I put through a request for a copy of Mrs. Adams's tax return. When it landed on my desk, all my vague doubts and suspicions suddenly jelled into a very specific certainty: I was up against a case of income-spreading, on an absolutely magnificent scale.

Mrs. Adams, according to her return, was not only age 65 or over, but blind. This gave her three personal exemptions. Her income was slightly under $7,000: roughly $4,000 from Joe the Detective, and the remainder from Social Security and a small annuity. With that low income and three exemptions, she paid very little tax.

I turned the case over to the intelligence division, and in time the whole story was revealed. Joe the Detective had the endearing habit of befriending elderly folks who were struggling along on starvation incomes. Having befriended an old pensioner and earned his trust, Joe would suggest a deal: At various times during the year, Joe would give the pensioner checks totaling about $4,000. The pensioner would cash them and give most of the cash back to Joe. The pensioner would keep enough money to pay the tax on his alleged $4,000 of income, and he would also keep perhaps $100 for himself—a lot of money to him, though not to Joe.

What Joe got out of the deal was the gorgeous advantage of having his high-middle income taxed as though it were nine separate near-poverty incomes.

He went to jail for criminal fraud. As for the old folks, apparently nobody at IRS had the heart to prosecute them.

The episode of Therapeutic Thelma began when a taxpayer named Henry, a bachelor, took a highly unusual medical deduction. The deduction totaled $600, and Henry reported it with his tax return as six separate payments of $100 to a certain "T. Wilkins." (For reasons that will become obvious, I use a fictitious name.) Since it didn't say "Dr. T. Wilkins" or "T. Wilkins, M.D.," I questioned the item.

"Who is this T. Wilkins, where does he live and what did he do for you?" I asked.

Henry seemed very nervous when he replied. "It's a she," he said. "Thelma."

"Well, okay, Thelma. What's she a doctor of?"

Henry swallowed uncomfortably. "She's a—well—a prostitute."

I invited Henry to explain.

He explained, with a good deal of stuttering, that he was afflicted with a sex problem. A psychoanalyst had advised him to practice certain techniques with a prostitute, in the hope that this might give him confidence to find a loving relationship with some other woman later. Henry showed me a letter from the psychoanalyst, addressed "To whom it may concern"—mainly, to IRS. The letter substantiated Henry's statement that he had visited T. Wilkins on professional advice and for therapeutic purposes.

I didn't know how to handle the problem. To buy time, I asked Henry to prove that he had actually paid Thelma $600.

"She wouldn't let me pay by check," he said. "She insisted on cash. So I had to substantiate the expense in a kind of roundabout way. I got her to talk to my analyst by phone, and—well, read this."

He handed me a second letter from the psychoanalyst. The letter said, "To whom it may concern: This will certify that I have spoken to Miss Wilkins by telephone, that she has performed the therapeutic services which I counseled for Mr. ———, that she performed the services on six occasions, and that her fee was one hundred dollars per act of service."

I was buffaloed. I decided I'd better go back to the office and talk to my chief.

He talked to his boss, who in turn talked to his. In the end I was sent back to see Henry and make a deal.

The thoughts of IRS were that Thelma, like most prostitutes, probably filed no tax returns. That was undoubtedly why she insisted on payment in cash: She wanted no records made of her name or income. She might actually have a very high income and a large store of wealth—lots of juice for IRS, if we could find it. More juice, certainly, than the relatively minor amount of extra tax we would collect by disallowing Henry's $600 medical deduction.

"So here is the deal," I told Henry. "You give me

Thelma's address, and give me a signed affidavit stating what you paid her, when and why. If you do that, you've got your deduction."

Henry thought it over for a couple of days, then agreed.

Special agents of the intelligence division took over from there. They discovered, by following Thelma around for a week, that she kept large checking accounts at three different banks. One special agent posed as an elevator operator in her high-priced apartment building. By counting the number of men who visited her over a one-week period, and by multiplying that number by 52 and then by $100, he arrived at an estimate of the annual income she was failing to report.

The only defense her lawyer could make stick in court was that she always took an eight-week summer vacation; therefore, IRS should multiply by 44, not 52.

We ended by extracting something like $90,000 from her three bank accounts. We were happy to let Henry have his $600 deduction. We felt we had struck an excellent bargain.

Generous George, an executive with an income near $70,000, declared a bad debt of $27,000. A computer shrieked with anguish, and I went around to see what the hell George was up to.

He was a tall, grey-haired gentleman, courtly, charming, reasonable. He said he could fully understand why his return had raised questions. He was, he said, prepared to substantiate his claim. "You will go away, sir, fully satisfied," he said.

I suggested he try me. All right: The $27,000, he said, was the total of a series of loans he had made over a long

period of years to his father. He had loaned the old gentleman a thousand bucks one year, four grand another year,
and so on. He gave me a sheaf of canceled checks. "You
will find," he said, "that these add up to precisely twenty-
seven thousand."

I added them. They did. I examined the faces of the
checks and the endorsements. They seemed bona fide.

"That's fine," I said. "What you have shown me so far
is that you handed twenty-seven thousand to your father,
beginning twelve years ago. What you haven't shown me
is that these were loans. When money changes hands between family members like this, we usually find it's a gift,
not a loan."

He nodded. "Yes, I am aware of that. But I can back
up my statement that this entire bundle of checks was a
loan. You see, my father was not a very practical man. He
was an inventor, something of a dreamer. He always
needed money to promote his inventions, but no bank
would lend him a dime. Since I had enjoyed a certain
amount of success in the world, I offered to be his bank,
up to a limit. We had an agreement under which he would
repay principal and interest—a very modest rate of interest
—if and when one of his inventions paid off. Some of his
ideas were excellent, and I thought my chances of being
repaid were quite good."

"But now you're satisfied he won't repay?" I asked.

"He died last year."

"Leaving no estate?"

"Absolutely flat broke. In debt, as a matter of fact."

I nodded and said, "So far, so good." The law says that
a debt becomes a bad debt, and hence a tax deduction, in
the year when it becomes finally and irrevocably uncollectable. The taxpayer must supply proof of this final un-

collectability. The death of the debtor, broke, is among the most convincing proofs. I said, "I suppose you can document that you'll get no repayment from your father's estate?"

"Absolutely."

"Okay, then we've got just one problem. Prove to me that this twenty-seven thousand was a loan."

George nodded. "I will. I was very careful about this from the beginning. Every time I handed my father a check, I had him give me a letter. Here are all the letters."

He handed me a neat, paper-clipped sheaf. The first letter, dated 12 years back, said, "Dear George: Thank you for the loan of $2,000. As we agreed, I will repay this loan, plus simple annual interest at 3%, at such time as . . ."

All the other letters were similar, except that each succeeding letter mentioned the cumulative total of the loan as it then stood. The letters were neatly typed on plain white paper, with the old gentleman's name and address rubber-stamped on top and his signature below.

I didn't quite know what to make of it. There is nothing in the Internal Revenue Code that says a son can't lend money to his dear old dad—nor that, in the event dad defaults, the son can't treat it like any other bad debt. And yet . . .

Something about the situation made me feel uncomfortable. It was the sixth sense of the battle-scarred revenue agent: the little warning buzzer in the back of his head that tells him he is being lied to.

I was absolutely certain Generous George was lying. I figured him for a careful man, so I knew every checkable fact would check out if I chose to challenge him. He would be able to prove that his father actually had been an inventor, that he actually had died broke, and so on. No matter how deeply I dug, all the tangible facts would turn out to be as George had stated them. But the $27,000? That, I was sure, was George's big lie. He had given that money to his father over the years, expecting no repayment. When the father died, George had suddenly been struck by an idea for a magnificent tax gimmick. He had typed those letters himself and forged his father's signature on them.

This was how I read the case. But how to prove it?

I told Generous George I would need to consult with my supervisor. I went back to my office with the sheaf of letters.

I spread the letters on my desk and looked at them. The oldest letter didn't look 12 years older than the most recent one, and that perhaps was why the warning buzzer had bleeped in my mind. The white paper of that allegedly 12-year-old letter was not yellowed, nor was the paper limp along the fold lines. George had been clever enough to dog-ear the corners and to make smudge marks on the paper, but it still didn't look old enough. That was a subjective impression, however; it wouldn't mean anything in court. Would a chemical analysis help me? I didn't know.

I looked at the signatures. George had been careful to vary the ink color from letter to letter, but beyond that the signatures looked remarkably alike. I recalled learning in one of my IRS indoctrination courses that a man's signature usually changes over the years, particularly when he gets old, and may change radically. I wondered if a handwriting analyst could contribute anything useful to the case.

With a vague idea of comparing signatures, I called for a few copies of the father's tax returns spanning the

12-year period. And by doing so, quite accidentally, I caught Generous George by the tail.

It turned out that George's father, in the second year of the 12-year period, had changed his address. George had evidently forgotten this damning little fact. The purported 12-year-old letter was rubber-stamped with an address to which his father had not moved until two years later.

George burst into tears when the special agents confronted him with this inconsistency. According to one agent who talked to me about the case later, George took the rubber stamp from his desk drawer, contemplated it morosely for a moment and hurled it through a screened window. The agent picked it up as he left, brought it back to the office and gave it to me. "Frame it," he suggested.

I couldn't figure out how, so I put it somewhere. Today, like many things around IRS, it is lost.

Half-a-Business Harry was a taxpayer who owned a large house, the expenses of which were eating him alive. Seeking financial help, he turned to the U.S. Treasury. He used a common gambit, the faked mail-order business conducted at home.

He rigged a couple of rooms in his house to look like offices. He invented a goofy product which he could pretend to sell, an astrological-prediction service of some kind. He didn't care whether the product sold or not—the main thing was to establish the appearance of a going business. If he could establish that, he could tax-deduct a portion of the depreciation, maintenance, heating and other costs of his home.

When I came around to audit him, he had just enough of a business going to make his case. His main income, about $45,000, came from his regular job as an airline pilot and from some stock-market investments. His fake mail-order business had produced a couple of hundred dollars of income.

"Frankly," I told him, "my instinct is to disallow most of this home-office cost. I don't see why you need two rooms to conduct two hundred dollars' worth of business."

He had shown me the two office rooms. He had them carefully littered with paper, books, file folders and other officelike paraphernalia. I knew damned well that the minute I left they would be returned to their normal use as bedrooms, TV rooms or whatever they really were.

Half-a-Business Harry shrugged. "Can I help it," he asked, "if my business isn't earning a fortune? You can't deny a man a business tax deduction just because his business isn't succeeding."

What he said was true. Still I went on arguing. "It doesn't look to me," I said, "like you're even trying to get this business off the ground. Hell, you've only shown me three small ads about your service. If you really wanted to sell the service, it seems to me you'd advertise it more."

"I'm starting small," said Harry, huffily. "I don't want to borrow. I can't spend any more than the business earns."

The tax court has upheld worse-faked businesses than his. I finally told Harry, "All right, I'll allow it this year. But let me give you a warning. If I come back next year and find you still aren't trying any harder than you are now, I'm going to guess your business is only a tax scheme."

This was sheer bluster. A revenue agent has no authority to decide who gets audited and who doesn't. He can suggest a follow-up audit, and sometimes his suggestion will be considered and sometimes it won't. But he can't predict in one year whom he will be auditing the next year.

Half-a-Business Harry took the threat seriously, however. He promised that if I came back the following year I would find the business either fully off the ground or dead.

I didn't audit him the following year. Then, about a year and a half after that first audit, I received a letter from Harry. It said: "I placed some more ads and got my business off the ground. The astrology service is selling better than I expected. It is selling so well that I had to quit my job and work at home full time. Thanks, you bastard."

But enough crazy stories. I will tell you more of them as we wander our way around, over, under and through the United States income tax. At the moment, I want to pause in my storytelling and do a little explaining and complaining.

Chapter 2

THE
REVENUE
AND
THE
AGENT

Before I go further, I think it will be useful for you to know something about the scheme and scope of things at the Internal Revenue Service. It will help you to see where I fit into that scheme and what my peculiar perspective is.

The Revenue Service at present has nearly 70,000 employees. Of these, about 4,500 work at Washington headquarters, and the rest work in that giant hunting preserve we call "the field." The bulk of our colossal army is made up of clerks, secretaries, computer folks and other types of workers found in any large organization whose principal business is to move pieces of paper around. In addition, there are several specialized breeds of field hunters who meet taxpayers face-to-face under various sad or happy circumstances, for various nice or nasty purposes. These are the breeds you will encounter in this book.

Our hunting preserve, the United States, is broken up for our purposes into seven regions and 58 districts. Each region is run by a commissioner, and each of these has seven assistant regional commissioners working for him. Each assistant regional commissioner runs one division, and the divisions are administration, appellate, alcohol-tobacco-firearms, data processing, audit, intelligence, and collection. The last three contain most of the field hunters, including myself, and these are the three that will crop up most often in the chapters to follow.

The audit division, as its name implies, contains the men and women who look over taxpayers' returns for errors, omissions and naughtiness.

Most audits conducted by this division are routine. A TP's return isn't selected for audit because he is suspected of having done wrong; it may be selected for any of a thousand reasons. Perhaps the TP has simply been swept up, by sheer chance, in a random sampling. Or perhaps IRS, in that year, has decided to concentrate on people in that taxpayer's profession, to find out whether they cheat any worse than people in other professions. Or perhaps a computer has selected the TP because his medical deductions are larger than what is considered normal for his family size and income bracket.

A taxpayer who receives a letter or phone call from this division, requesting the pleasure of his company at an audit, need not feel or behave like a suspected criminal. He can assume he is under no suspicion at all. His return is merely being checked, and although the audit may be a damned nuisance it will not normally be a prosecutor-and-defendant proceeding.

The men (and in recent years women) who conduct audits for this division are called *office auditors* and *revenue agents*. The former stay at desks in their district or local offices. They deal mainly with the simpler kinds of tax returns, principally the returns of lower- and middle-income salaried folks and wage earners.

Revenue agents are higher paid and more often go out to beard taxpayers in their dens. They are often, though unofficially, called *field agents*. Among them: me.

This doesn't mean I spend all my time drifting around in the field. I conduct office audits, too. Within certain limits, it's my choice to make. At most local and district offices, a field agent is left pretty much on his own in this and other respects. His work is subject to review, of course, and he works against unwritten but clearly understood quotas in terms of the number of cases he closes and the amount of new tax money he brings in. But I can decide for myself when, where and how to conduct any given audit. If I feel an audit will be quick and simple, or if I'm feeling lazy, I ask the taxpayer to come to me. If I feel like getting out of the office, I go to the taxpayer. In the summer especially, field agents like to find quick audits that they can conduct in the afternoons. Finding himself far from his own office and with an audit completed at four o'clock, an agent can quite easily argue himself into going home.

The intelligence division concentrates on cases of suspected tax fraud. If a revenue agent like me starts an audit and stumbles across what looks like evidence of provable fraud, he stops auditing. He turns the case over to the i telligence division. He may be asked to continue working on the case, since he is presumed to know more about it in the beginning than anybody else, but it is no longer his baby. The case has officially passed from the audit division's jurisdiction to the intelligence division's.

The principal hunters of the intelligence division are called *special agents.* Their Civil Service classifications and pay are the same as revenue agents', but the educational requirements are somewhat different (a revenue agent needs more accountancy credits), and the approach to the taxpayer is different. If you receive a letter or phone call from a special agent, you can guess you are involved in a fraud investigation.

Some special agents concentrate on substantially the same kind of number-juggling work that a revenue agent does. They examine books, poke through bank and stockbroker records and so on. Others lead lives of somewhat more intrigue. They may work undercover, posing as dope pushers or gamblers or barflies. They get into such interesting work as listening in on people's phone conversations and opening people's mail—which is illegal, but sure brings in the tax money. These are the types of IRS employees who turn up in television dramas. Once in a while a revenue agent will do similar cloak-and-dagger work, though it is not usual.

The collection division, as its name says, collects. Most of this work is routine. In fact, it may be the most mind-bendingly routine work on the face of the earth. It consists mainly of opening envelopes. But there are always taxpayers who fail to pay up—fail to send checks with their returns, or fail to come up with the extra tax recommended by agents such as myself. At any given moment the national backlog of "delinquent accounts" is between $1.5 billion and $2 billion. Part of the collection division's mandate is to go out and squeeze all those delinquent taxpayers until they give up the juice.

The special breed of hunter who does this work is called a *revenue officer*. He generally starts by sending the delinquent TP a polite (but stiff) note full of organizational phrases such as "we would call to your attention" and "a review of your account discloses." If this doesn't shake the TP, a coolly courteous phone call may be next, followed by a distinctly less courteous phone call or a personal visit. As a last resort, the revenue officer has the administrative license to seize the victim's bank account, garnishee his wages, drive off with his car, take over and padlock his place of business or otherwise summarily deprive him of property and the pursuit of happiness.

Young law or accountancy students newly recruited into the Revenue Service are often trained initially as revenue officers. Some like the work and stay in it. Others find themselves having nightmares about it—"Please, Mr. Officer, don't take my baby's crib too!"—and eventually request transfer to other duties. Many become revenue agents or special agents.

These are the principal hunters who stalk taxpayers in the field. As a taxpayer you may also meet certain other IRS folks on occasion. There are the taxpayer service representatives who help people with their returns as the April 15 climax approaches. And there are the internal security agents of the inspection service. They stalk other agents stalking taxpayers. If you ever feel you have been pushed around unfairly, bullied, subjected to an extortion attempt, illegally spied upon or otherwise mistreated by an

IRS employee, you will be invited to weep on the shoulder of an internal security man, generally known in IRS as an inspector or house dick.

Even though there are almost 70,000 of us in this monster of a hunting club, our number is too small for the job we are assigned to do. The body of law with which we must deal is enough by itself to overwhelm us. I feel quite safe in saying there is no one man or woman in IRS who knows the whole tax law. Indeed, you could probably pick any ten of us at random and the entire group would score less than 100% on a test dealing with the law's finer points.

The *Wall Street Journal* perpetrated a mean hoax in 1972: It sent a reporter around to five different IRS offices with the same relatively simple tax return. The five offices came up with five different answers about the amount of tax owed. The offices not only disagreed on the final figure, but on the computational steps used to arrive at the figure, on the number of forms to be filled out and on almost everything else except the date when the return was due. They all said April 15.

The sheer physical size of the job is also overwhelming. In the fiscal year ended June 30, 1971, we took in $192 billion from all tax sources, including $101 billion from individual income taxes. We processed 111 million returns of all types. We mathematically verified 73 million of them and examined or audited more than 1.5 million of them. We mailed out 56 million refund checks totaling $19 billion. We received some 360 million information forms and reports.

We nearly drowned in paper.

Chapter 3

RICH MAN, POOR MAN, MIDDLEMAN...

A revenue agent is something like a dentist. People may grudgingly recognize he is doing a job that needs to be done, but they don't like him much while he is doing it.

They wonder why any sane man would enter a profession that wins him so little affection. In the dentist's case, one good answer is money. Many dentists grow moderately rich, and a few—especially those with good tax advice—grow immoderately rich. But a revenue agent can grow rich only by habitually accepting bribes. His salary may rise into the high teens if he is lucky, behaves himself, sticks with the job long enough. He can't even cheat much on his income tax, for his returns are scrutinized more thoroughly and regularly than any other middle-income citizen's. Money? No. If you want money you become a dentist, not a revenue man. Affection? Love?

Smiles? If those are the main rewards you seek from your work, you probably don't become either a dentist or a revenue man. But the dentist has an advantage. When he hangs up his drill and his white coat, he becomes just folks. Out of the office, people respond to him for what he is, not what he does professionally. At cocktail parties they don't talk to him with their lips compressed, fearing that he secretly wishes to examine their teeth for defects. A revenue agent never quite wins this degree of relaxed acceptance. People see him coming and say, "Oh, oh! Revenue! Gotta watch what I say. . . ." His presence makes people nervous. He closes conversational doors. People enjoy telling each other about successful tax-cheating methods they've used, but when the agent comes around they talk about the weather.

Then why am I a revenue agent?

I thought I knew long ago, when I was younger, but I'm not sure anymore. When I was younger, there was something about the federal government itself that attracted me. I suppose I had visions of myself helping to make history or something. The fellow who recruited me from a college campus pointed out, too, that a job with the Internal Revenue Service could offer wide-ranging practical experience, an excellent continuing education for a young accountancy major. The starting pay wasn't bad compared with what private industry was offering. The recruiter added, truthfully, that IRS was a good outfit to work for in terms of job security, fringe benefits, a large and fatherly love for its huge family of employees. Moreover, as the recruiter carefully failed to point out, I could guess the job would bring me into contact with business firms that might offer me higher pay after I gained experience. So I thought, all right, what the hell. And I went through a brief training course and bought myself some white shirts and a briefcase and became a revenue agent.

Today I am less than content. It isn't the low pay that troubles me particularly. If money were my sole object I would long ago have skulked into a $50,000-a-year sinecure in private industry. Revenue agents get juicy job offers in the course of auditing corporate tax accounts. The bigger the tax deficiency that seems to be looming up, the bigger the job. But money isn't my main problem. Nor does the nature of the work itself cause me inordinate pain. Sure, I would rather be out in my boat than trudging around with my briefcase, but if I've got to work, this is the kind of work I like. I get some kind of aesthetic satisfaction from making sets of figures balance out. Nutty, you say? Well, to each his own insanity. Some people like poetry, some like engines, some like numbers.

No, the salary doesn't offend me and the work doesn't bore me. What troubles me is the environment of law in which I must work. As a revenue agent I am a kind of policeman. My job, condensed to its essential nugget of fact, is law enforcement. My problem is that I don't like the law I am employed to enforce.

This is obviously an untenable position for a policeman to be in. An exquisitely painful position, sometimes. So I don't know where I go from here. I think I should probably stick around to see what becomes of the tax reforms that are now being talked about in Washington. History gives me no sound reason to be optimistic about these promised reforms. There have been dozens of "reforms" since the first U.S. income-tax law of 1913, but no reform has yet accomplished anything more than to make the law more complicated. I am not optimistic, but I cling to a handful of hope. I will wait. And if the new reforms don't reform, I will leave.

The worst feature of the law—the feature that makes me a reluctant enforcer—is the great, crushing pressure it puts on the middle class. I am keenly aware that it is unfashionable to say this, but I like middle-class Americans more than anybody else. In our era of strident advocacy of this cause and that, they are the ones who bellyache the least. Hardly anyone has said anything nice about them since the 1950s, when they were applauded for supplying most of the energy behind the nation's fantastic postwar economic boom. Since then they have been dropped from favor like a gang of builders who having erected a fine palace are kicked out the back door. Campus liberals, literary intellectuals and dozens of other groups hoot at them constantly from the palace windows. Yet I think the time has come for some serious national thinking about their money problems, particularly problems caused by the income tax. Middle-income people need sympathy and need it badly.

The rich have problems, I'm told, but I must assume they can take care of their problems by themselves. The poor also have problems, quite obviously, but income taxation is one problem they don't have. If you are living in poverty, we sympathetic folks at IRS will collect no money from you, or, if we collect some through withholding during the year, we will refund it almost cheerfully. Thus, at the risk of seeming callous, I will have to say that the problems of the poor are beyond the scope of this book.

In any case, I am a man of few tears. That is a requirement of the revenue agent's job. Great torrents of tears have been shed for the poor in the past several lachrymose years, and if I were to pour my meager cupful into this salty flood, nobody would notice the difference. It seems to me that my tears, when I shed any, can be shed more usefully for the income group that hasn't been watered enough.

Consider the middle-income man and his relationship to the tax law. The law says each citizen should pay a tax that is proportionate to his ability to pay. That is fair. Even noble, perhaps. The difficulty is that graduated income taxes, including ours in America, have never worked in practice according to the grand and laudable designs set down on paper. What always happens—what has happened in every nation that has ever set up a graduated income tax—is that the highest *actual* rates are paid by the middle class.

The poor, as we've noted (and this is the last time we'll note it), pay little or no income tax. The law says they shouldn't, and in their case the law works. But, frustratingly, the rich also escape taxes to an enormous extent. They do it in many ways, which we'll examine in more detail later, but primarily they do it by having the economic oomph to influence legislation in their favor; by having the financial maneuverability to wriggle through what we grinningly call loopholes (wider than barn doors, some of them); by being able to afford the smartest lawyers and tax accountants; by being able to bribe with effect.

What can a middle-income taxpayer do? A middle-income TP, as we like to call him at IRS, can do hardly anything except pay the tax rates stated in the official tables. Or he can cheat. But we'll take up that intriguing subject a little later.

The official tax tables currently show a noble progression of percentages going up to 70% for incomes over $100,000. The fact is that hardly anybody pays 70% or anything like it. The further fact is that the highest actual rates are paid by salaried people in the upper-middle range, say from about $30,000 to $50,000 a year. Salary and wage earners in the range of $15,000 to $30,000 pay less, but are still socked more heavily than are large numbers of millionaires. I've audited many $100,000-a-year men who paid smaller percentages than lower-middle TPs in the $8,000-to-$15,000 bracket. I've audited a man whose income was over $500,000 and whose total tax for the year was $58. He wasn't cheating. It was legal.

Now, understand me. I don't want to deny the rich their fun. I would love to be rich and enjoy the fun myself. Yet it must be remembered that the nation needs a certain amount of tax money each year to keep its colossal machinery running. IRS hauls in nearly $200 billion a year from all tax sources, and not even that stunning amount is enough, for the federal budget still shows deficits. Perhaps federal spending can be cut and the deficits written out, but there is still a minimum need for revenue, and the minimum is huge and inexorably rising. If the rich don't come up with their share, who must be asked to make up the difference? The poor? Of course not. As usual, the man in the middle.

The U.S. "graduated" income tax of the 1970s is not a new development in history. As far as I know, every graduated income tax on earth has degenerated thus from its original high purposes. Degeneration seems to be built into the very meat and bones of income taxation, just as aging and bodily decay and eventual death are built into the future of every human at birth. There seems to be no way to dodge this baffling fact.

The essential truths are that income taxation deals with money, and money equals power, and those with that power will always seek ways to sidestep income taxation. Or to put it another way, the more heavily a man is supposed to be taxed, the more power he has to escape being taxed. Diogenes' Dictum. The Patrician Paradox. Call it what you will, it has arisen to confound all the graduated income taxes in history.

Sir Walter Scott was an early victim of the graduated income tax's cruel effect. More than one and a half centuries ago, he wrote a poem about a sultan named Solimaun who was laid low by a seizure of intractable melancholy. Solimaun's physicians advised him that the best hope of a cure lay in finding a perfectly happy man. Combing the world for a therapeutic individual of this rare type, the sad sultan heard rumors that John Bull of England might fill the prescription. Unfortunately the rumors were wrong. Asked about his emotional state, John Bull roared:

> Happy? Why, cursed war and racking tax
> Have left us scarcely raiment to our backs!

The "cursed war" that troubled John Bull was the war against Napoleon, and the "racking tax" that caused him such pain—and also pained Scott personally—was the world's first formal graduated income tax. Enacted in 1799, its rates were endearingly modest by today's standards: from less than 1% to a top rate of 10%. But Walter Scott—poet, novelist, lawyer, literary promoter, real-estate speculator—had the misfortune in his peak years to earn an income that put him just barely into the top bracket, and this enraged him. He was not a member of the comfortably wealthy class; toward the end of his life, in fact, he slid into debt. In terms of his living standard and the general weight and tone of his money worries, his economic status was roughly analogous to what we would call upper middle today. He felt that people of his economic group were the worst "racked" of all. "If the tax rate is to proceed upward in steps," he wrote once to his publishing partner, James Ballantyne, "why must I, though not wealthy, be placed on the top floor?" He thought the wealthy should be made to pay more than he.

They should have been—and, were it not for the facts set forth in Diogenes' Dictum, would have been. In planning that granddaddy of all graduated income taxes, members of Parliament and other officials talked a lot of pious talk about "ability to pay" and all that, the standard pronouncements that politicians always use when planning new income taxes or promising to reform old ones. It seemed proper to those fair-minded Britons of the late 1790s that the richest citizens should pay the highest percentage rates. What they excluded from their calculations, or chose not to announce in public, was that the richest wouldn't want to pay the highest rates and couldn't be made to do so. When the time came to set the rates of graduation, the influential wealthy saw to it that the top rate was set at the upper-middle income level. This had the effect of shifting the tax burden downward, so that a man like Scott paid considerably more than he would have if the wealthy had been taxed more heavily. Any middle-class TP in modern America knows exactly how Scott felt when he wrote of cursed war and racking tax.

About half a century after Scott wrote those timeless words, another articulate man arose to shed a tear for the taxpayer in the middle. He was William Graham Sumner, an Episcopal minister and a distinguished professor of political and social science at Yale. This combination of vocations apparently gave him a special perspective. He advocated prayer as a means of solving problems, but he also appreciated the fact that a few dollars could be a big help too.

His favorite people were those a couple of notches above the poverty level, people in what we would probably call the lower-middle income group. These people, he sadly pointed out, earned just enough money so that nobody (except Sumner) felt sorry for them. Unlike the poor, they were expected to make their own way through life with no help from governments or charitable institutions. Unlike the rich, they barely had the means to make their way and tended to die early of overwork.

Sumner gave a famous speech in 1883. He talked about what he called the forgotten man, "delving away in patient industry, supporting his family, paying his taxes, casting his vote, supporting the church and the school. . . . His chief business in life is to pay." To pay for everything and everybody. To provide welfare for the poor and tax breaks for the rich. To support communities, states, the nation and also, it often seems, much of the rest of the world too.

Do you have the feeling that your chief business in life is to pay? Then you are a middle-income TP, and I fondly dedicate this book to you.

Chapter 4

I remarked earlier that cheating generates fun. Unfortunately, it also generates tears, and the tears prevent me from enjoying the game as much as I might. I feel obliged, therefore, to register a complaint against the system that allows cheating to flourish so freely, the foolish and maybe immoral system we call voluntary compliance.

I once met a taxpayer who in the untidy attic of my memory is filed under the name Honest John. He filed his 1040 one year with a check for about $400, representing the balance of his year's income tax as he figured it. Six months later he filed an amended return, 1040X, asking for most of his $400 back. A couple of weeks after that he filed still another 1040X saying forget it, he didn't want the $400 back after all. I went out to see what the hell he thought he was doing.

There is nothing wrong with filing an amended return; we receive hundreds of thousands of them every year. The law says that with certain exceptions you can file an amended return and claim a refund within three years of the date when your original return was due. That is, if you file your 1973 return on or before the deadline of April 15, 1974, and if you then discover you've made a mistake and paid too much tax, we'll give you until April 15, 1977, to hit us for a refund. In the unlikely event you want to tell us you've paid too little tax—that is, you want to pay *more*—we'll give you from now until doomsday to file an amended return. You can use either the special 1040X or a plain 1040.

No, amended returns aren't uncommon. But it is uncommon to find a man filing an amendment to an amendment, and that is why I called on Honest John.

He was a rotund, bald fellow with a face like a big red apple. He earned his main income as a computer engineer, but he was also greatly interested in gambling. He was a sucker for lotteries and he also played poker for fairly high stakes nearly every weekend. The problems that caused him to double-amend his return arose from this gambling avocation.

He told me the story with a frankness I found unusual among taxpayers. He sat there, looked me in the eye and admitted that he had attempted to cheat.

The episode began when he won a car in a lottery conducted by a men's service club. In making out his original tax return, he declared the car's value of roughly $1,500 as income, as the law requires. In his tax bracket, this upped his liability by about $400.

Somewhat later he realized that the club running the lottery had never sent him a copy of a 1099 information return. Under the law, the club was supposed to have mailed such a return to IRS, stating the value of the prize and the name of the winner. Honest John went around to see the treasurer of the club, and the treasurer said, "Why, no, we never did send in a 1099. We forgot all about it. I thought of it once, but I had my own taxes to worry about and I just decided the hell with it." (Many people and organizations decide the hell with it. The penalty for failing to file a 1099 is, in most cases, ten bucks.)

Honest John thus learned that he had declared $1,500 of income which, if he had kept quiet, might have stayed hidden. He mentioned this at one of his weekend poker games. Many of his friends around the table opined that he had been a damned fool. One man in particular urged Honest John to file an amended return and get his money back.

"But how?" Honest John asked. "I've already declared the $1,500. How can I undeclare it?"

His friend asked, "How did you declare it? I mean, what kind of income did you call it?"

John replied that he had entered the $1,500 on Schedule E, Supplemental and Miscellaneous Income. He had labeled the amount "gambling winnings."

"Then you're home free!" exulted the friend. "For all IRS knows, 'gambling winnings' could be poker pots, right? So all you do is file an amended return saying you just learned you're allowed to deduct gambling *losses* from gambling winnings. You play dumb, see? You didn't know the law till all us clever guys read it to you. You tell IRS you won fifteen hundred bucks one month, but you lost two grand another month, something like that. The loss cancels out the gain."

John's other friends thought this was a dandy idea.

Hardly anything is more fun than putting one over on the Revenue Service. "We'll back you up, John baby!" they all said with huge enthusiasm.

Honest John decided against the idea, then for it, then against it. When he had vacillated for several weeks, his friends began calling him a sucker. "Everybody else cheats on taxes, John," they pointed out (not quite accurately— "everybody" is hyperbolic; "the majority" is accurate). So finally Honest John succumbed. He mailed off an amended return and undeclared his $1,500 of gambling winnings.

"But then I began to get unhappy," he told me, finishing his story. "I was miserable, if you want to know the truth. Couldn't sleep nights. Drank too much. Indigestion too. My God, you wouldn't believe the indigestion. So in the end my wife asks me, 'John, is the lousy four hundred worth all this misery?' And I tell her, 'No, you're right.' So I end up by sending a new amended return to cancel out the first one."

"And now you feel better?" I asked.

Honest John was nothing if not honest. He said, "No. Now I feel like a goddam fool."

Our commissioners of Internal Revenue have always pointed with pride to the voluntary-compliance system. Each April, in the bittersweet spring, you will find a solemn Message from the Commissioner on the front of your tax-forms booklet. The message always makes some pleased reference to voluntary compliance. It says things like, "97% of all Americans pay their taxes voluntarily," and "this is a real compliment to our American system," and "we pledge a vigorous enforcement against the very few who would attempt to cheat the system." I even have a book in my library, written by two men of absolutely amazing faith, which says "99.999 percent of American taxpayers are honest."

It sounds beautiful. Visiting foreign taxation specialists are always amazed by it. At least, they are always courteous enough to say they're amazed. Imagine! A nation of nearly 200 million people so honest, so upright, so patriotic that nearly all of them pay their taxes to the last cent, *voluntarily!* Can it really be?

No, it can't. The system of "taxation by confession," as a federal judge once called it, is a cruel lie and a dirty trick. I'll discuss the lie first, and then I'll explain why I use that mean little phrase, "dirty trick."

There is no need to be unnecessarily cynical, but let's at least be realistic. A favorite saying among the spacecraft folk at Cape Kennedy is: "If something can go wrong, it probably will." Diogenes' Second Dictum is a partial plagiarism of that statement. The dictum reads: If a taxpayer thinks he can cheat safely, he probably will.

And why not? We are not talking about cheating in a neighborhood card game. We are talking about economic survival. The two situations are different by several orders of magnitude. It is easy to be honest in a card game. In fact, an act of conspicuous honesty can fill you with a warm glow of pleasure and self-congratulation. You tell your opponent to hold his cards closer so you can't see them. He thanks you. You feel good. But that is only a game. If you lose, it won't hurt. Not enough to make you desperate, at any rate.

But the struggle for economic survival is not a game, especially in the 1970s. The average middle-income TP when he mails off his tax return each April 15 is mailing a document that will profoundly affect his own and his family's welfare. He is fighting to keep his frail economic ship afloat in a raging sea of rising prices, rising interest rates, rising taxes of all kinds. He may be in a chronically half-drowned state. Each time he pulls his battered craft through an economic difficulty, another huge wave is already smashing on his bow. He may be desperate—many middle-income people are. If he can save a couple of hundred bucks by cheating on his income tax, and if he badly needs the money to pay a doctor bill or a late mortgage installment, can you blame him if he cheats?

Perhaps you can. I can't. If I audit his return and discover his transgression I will make him pay up, of course—my job requires me to do that. But I will not give him any lectures about honesty. My job doesn't require lectures. As a matter of fact the Revenue Service—which is really a kindly outfit at heart, though it is forced to administer bad laws—specifically instructs its agents to avoid morality as a topic of discussion during audits.

I hold morality to be relative. It might be wrong to cheat in a game, and it would certainly be silly. It is less wrong and far less silly to cheat when your economic survival is at stake. Indeed, it may not be wrong at all in the sense of abstract morality. This is a competitive world. We are all fighting against our environment and against each other, and it seems strange to set up moralistic rules that forbid us to use certain weapons, at least in the battle for financial survival. Animals in the wild have no concepts of morality. They take what they can get in any way they can get it. Survival is the only criterion. Only humans have dared pretend there is something more important than survival.

Your concept of morality may be more rigid than mine. But I believe it would become somewhat less rigid if you could accompany me on a year's round of tax audits.

You would see grown men with tears streaming down their cheeks. "My God, I can't pay it!" sobbed one debt-sunk middle-income salesman when I hit him with a $600 deficiency. "Where will I get it? What can I do?" I didn't know what he could do. That would be up to the revenue officer—the collection-division man—who would come around later to shovel up the money. Maybe the revenue officer would be sympathetic and let the devastated TP pay in installments. Maybe he would even declare the amount uncollectable—fifty-three it, as we say at IRS. I hoped for such an outcome, though I had no control over it. But I knew I didn't want to see the man punished any more for his attempt to cheat. I understood with poignant clarity why he had tried to cut $600 off his tax bill. In his position, I would have done the same.

And so would most other taxpayers. There are few Honest Johns among us. The fact is, the number of taxpayers who cheat is far greater than the publicized "few," the shifty-eyed "3%." I will offer some statistics later, but for the moment let me simply give you a guess based on my experience as a revenue agent. My guess is that at least half of all taxpayers and probably more have cheated at some time during their taxpaying careers. Some cheat regularly; some only when they need to. Some cheat timidly; some with magnificent arrogance. Some cheat grandiosely; some only in minor ways, by padding expense accounts, overstating doctor bills, failing to report little bits of cash income here and there. No matter. The point is that our tax laws are set up so that cheating is possible, and Diogenes' Second Dictum holds that what is possible will usually happen. It seems foolish to keep up the pretense that voluntary compliance works. Not only foolish, but unfair and perhaps even immoral. Let me tell you now why

I think the whole voluntary-compliance business is a dirty trick.

First, it is unfair to put a man in a high-pressure situation from which he can escape only by cheating, then order him not to cheat while simultaneously giving him the opportunity to do so. The strain on the man's moral fiber is too great, as Honest John discovered. It is cruel to torment him thus. It is like putting a gorgeous thick steak in front of a starving man. The commissioner's sweet little April 15 message says to the man, in effect, "It is against the law to touch that steak, and only a few people of low moral caliber would do such a despicable thing. Most people are of such high moral caliber that we've got a system of voluntary compliance around here. We aren't going to watch you. We know we can trust you. Your own honesty will make you do the right thing." So after a while when the fellow eats the steak, he feels guilty, miserable and scared, but what else can he do?

I don't know whose idea of fairness it is to torment people this way. The ordinary middle-income TP, hounded by costs that are rising faster than his income, is in the exact position of the starving man contemplating the forbidden steak, and the government each spring makes him submit to a cruel test of his moral strength. In the privacy of his home on the night of April 14, slumped over his Form 1040 in the annual act of confession, he thinks of many things. It occurs to him, as it did to Honest John, that a lot of other people are cheating. He has read about big-scale tax frauds in the newspapers. On his commuter train last week he sat next to a fellow who bragged about a dishonest tax gimmick that was saving him a grand a year. He glances at the pile of overdue bills on the corner of his desk. He wonders if the GMAC collection agent will phone him again tomorrow. He starts to enter his exemptions on the top of his tax form, and then hesitates. He thinks, "What if I say I've got four kids instead of three? Will they find out? Or what if. . . ?" But then he stops himself and says, "No, George, no! Be honest! Pay your share!" This gives him a warm little glow for a moment, until it occurs to him that nobody else will know he is honest.

This is no card game. No act of conspicuous honesty is possible. Tax returns are prepared in private, and each man's thoughts about taxes are also private. It would avail the honest TP nothing to go around shouting, "I didn't cheat!" Some might believe him; most wouldn't. Not even the revenue agent who audited his return would necessarily believe him.

What makes the middle-income taxpayer's agony still worse—and this is a second reason why the concept of voluntary compliance seems like a dirty trick—is that there are various degrees of opportunity to cheat. Degrees of opportunity obviously can't be measured precisely, like degrees of temperature, but to sort them out in my mind I like to think of them in broad categories. There are three degrees of cheating opportunity: small, large and total. (These categories could presumably be broken down further, and we could talk about "medium-large" and "large as hell" and so on, but why bother? The three main categories are enough to illustrate my point.)

In the *small-opportunity* class is the ordinary middle-class man or woman whose income is in the form of a wage or salary. In a typical year this taxpayer works for only one employer. The employer withholds taxes from the TP's paychecks all year long. At the end of the year the employer sends IRS a W-2 form saying exactly how much income the employee earned and how much tax was withheld. The employee has no chance to underdeclare this income. For him, "voluntary compliance" isn't all that voluntary. If he is in a mood to cheat, he must usually seek other, more difficult approaches than the simple failure to report income.

Large opportunity: a doctor, for example. His main income is in the form of small checks and cash payments from scores, perhaps hundreds, of patients. He knows many of these patients will report these payments on their own tax returns in the process of claiming medical deductions, but he also knows IRS lacks the manpower to cross-check his own tax return against those of all his patients. If he wants to cheat, he can cheat on a grand scale by reporting only half his actual income. His chances of getting away with it are good. Moreover, unlike the typical salaried employee, a self-employed professional like a doctor can cheat grandiosely by such means as claiming rental costs for an office that doesn't exist, claiming automobile costs for several thousand miles he didn't travel and so on.

Total opportunity: a call girl, for example. Her entire professional income is in the form of cash payments from men who will never report those payments to anybody. Not only could she cheat magnificently and with perfect safety if she filed a tax return, but the odds are she won't even bother to file at all. She need pay no income tax, ever. The chances that she will be caught are slim.

The law, in other words, discriminates unfairly against the wage or salary earner. It puts him into a situation where cheating is common and perhaps nearly universal, but it restricts his cheating opportunities while opening the door for other taxpayers.

It seems to me that if we are to have voluntary compliance at all, it should be as voluntary for one man as for another. Everyone's confessions should be trusted equally. But since I am convinced the whole idea is nonsense to begin with, I prefer to toy with the possibility of a non-voluntary system, a more cynical system that would place only the bare minimum of trust in personal honesty. More cynical—but also more fair.

My ideas about this hypothetical system are not very thoroughly developed. They may turn out to be only mad dreams. But I am sure that if enough people did enough thinking, we could invent something better than what we have now. I'll discuss such mad dreams later in the book.

I promised some statistics in support of my statement about the incidence of cheating. Here they are:

Consider, for example, the statistics on mathematical verification. This is a process in which returns are checked for simple internal consistency. No questions are asked about the TP's statements of his income or deductions. He is assumed, for the moment, to have stated all those figures accurately and truthfully. (Well, no, that isn't quite correct. We don't really assume he is honest; we merely allow a computer to assume it temporarily.) We then go over the TP's return to make sure that given the figures he has supplied he has performed all the internal computations correctly.

It is to be expected, of course, that large numbers of people will make mistakes in arithmetic. To expect otherwise would be to put too much trust in the tired human brain on the night of April 14. Of the 73 million returns that the Revenue Service checked arithmetically in fiscal 1971, slightly more than 4.5 million turned out to contain errors. There is nothing noteworthy about that. Some people are better at math (and at understanding tax instructions) than others. But if these were purely random errors, the laws of probability would suggest that about half the errors should be in the government's favor and the other half in the taxpayers'. Does this happen? No. Of those 4.5 million erroneous returns, some 3 million contained "mistakes" in the taxpayers' favor, and only 1.5 million in the government's.

Not only that, but the average protaxpayer error was considerably larger than the average progovernment error. As a result of mathematical verification, IRS found it owed $140 million in refunds to taxpayers who had paid too much. It billed $313 million to those who had paid too little.

Or take the statistics on audits. Of the 1.5 million returns examined by auditors and agents that year, a million —two-thirds—showed deficiencies. The dollar total of those deficiencies was almost $3.5 billion. Not million. *Billion.*

There's more to the story than that. Though one-third of the examinations failed to turn up deficiencies, this doesn't necessarily mean that all those half-million returns were prepared with scrupulous honesty. It means only that the examining agents couldn't spot or prove any errors or tricks.

As I have said, and as I will demonstrate in greater detail later, there are many ways to cheat and get away with it. Revenue agents often develop a kind of mental radar that signals the presence of skulduggery, but they are not really gifted with extrasensory perception. Most of them are at least moderately bright, but some taxpayers are brighter. No agent is infallible. It happens at least once a week that I walk out of an audit with a strong suspicion that I've been had, but with no practical way to prove it. In many cases—stock-market manipulations are a prime example—I will let a taxpayer get away because the task of proving my suspicions will take too much time. I work against quotas and I've got to concentrate on cases that promise the most juice for the smallest expenditure of days and hours. I am also perfectly sure that many taxpayers each year hoodwink me completely. They may cheat on a magnificent scale, but I go away from the examination with no suspicions; with nothing, perhaps, except the vague and uncomfortable sensation of a question mark somewhere in the back of my mind.

Those 1.5 million audited returns may or may not be a reliable sample of all returns. Some were selected for audit at random. Most were selected for specific reasons and purposes by a computer process we call the Discriminant Function System, or Dif for short. Dif picks out returns which, in its electronic opinion, have the highest likelihood of error or cheating and the biggest promise of juice.

Dif is clever, but I doubt that it's quite as clever as its creators fondly proclaim. There are many types of cheating gambits that can't be foiled in a routine way by either a computer or a human auditor. Such gambits can be defeated only in a random way: An agent just happens to see something that makes him suspicious; just happens to feel further probing will pay off; just happens to find the essential evidence that will make the case stick. It is perfectly possible to file a tax return that is one solid lie from beginning to end, but that Dif will ignore because all the stated facts and internal relationships fall within established boundaries which Dif has been instructed to consider safe. There are certain types of hidden income, for example, that defy detection either by electronics or by human eye and brain. And of course neither Dif nor IRS's human army has any good way of finding the hundreds of thousands of income earners (nobody knows how many there are) who never file tax returns at all.

Maybe there is far less general cheating than turns up on these selected returns, or maybe there is far more than is dreamt of in Dif's philosophy. Just for fun, however, let's suppose that the statistical biases cancel each other out and that the sample has something to tell us about tax-payers in general.

According to the sample, two-thirds of individual, corporate and institutional TPs in a given year pay less than they owe, and the average deficiency is $3,500 per return. Applying these figures to the 111 million returns filed in 1971, we come up with the guess that 74 million of them were deficient, to the tune of $259 billion. IRS collected only $192 billion. If this guesswork is correct, it means the tax haul was less than half of what it should have been.

But let's construct a more conservative estimate. Let's say the sample of selected returns is biased much too heavily in the direction of higher incomes and more complicated financial affairs. Let's guess further that the average deficiency per erroneous or fraudulent return is only $500, or one-seventh of the average shown in the sample. And let's guess that only half of all returns are deficient, rather than two-thirds. We still end with the shocking possibility that IRS should have collected $28 billion more than actually came in.

But this is all sheer guesswork. I suspect the figure of $28 billion is too low, but I have no way to prove it. I feel intuitively that the $259-billion figure is much too high, but I can't prove that either, and for all I know the true figure could be still higher. Such a possibility numbs the mind.

It is entirely conceivable, of course, that I labor under a heavy personal bias. My job as a revenue agent is to audit taxpayers fingered by Dif. If Dif is really so clever as to pick mainly the worst apples, my view of the tree may be skewed. There may be many more sound apples than I dream. It may even be, as visiting foreign officials have been polite enough to say, that Americans are the world's most honest and docile taxpayers. Yet I hope I will be forgiven for doubting it. What is more likely to be true is that American tax commissioners have better public-relations staffs than those of other nations. In France and Italy, tax avoidance and evasion are national games, played with gusto. In America we play the same games but talk about them less.

You must have guessed by now why I call myself Diogenes. Diogenes was an Athenian philosopher, a member of the Cynic school. According to a probably apocryphal legend, he walked about Athens carrying a lantern in broad daylight. Asked why, he replied grumpily (so says the legend) that he was looking for an honest man.

He was not really as sour a cynic as that story makes him seem. He didn't expect the worst from people. He believed only that there is a limit to the pressures any man can stand or the temptations he can ignore. Some have higher limits than others, but all have limits. This being so, Diogenes felt it was pointless to talk of "honesty" as though it might be a rigid structural member built into a man like a stone pillar, unbendable, eternally resistant to all the elements. Diogenes was saying only that people are made of flesh and blood, not stone.

There is no reason to suppose people have changed since Diogenes made his observations. I have never met a taxpayer made of stone. Nor a revenue agent either.

Let it be remembered that our nation was born largely because Americans hated taxation. Hated it so much that we were the last of all great Western nations to adopt an income tax. Have we changed so much since then?

Chapter 5

THROUGH HISTORY WITH THE TAX MAN

There has never been a government that could operate without money or its equivalent in goods and work. In ancient times some governments were apparently able to keep going for a while by forcibly extracting wealth and slaves from neighboring nations. But these aberrant and prosperous periods never lasted long, and in the end every government was obliged to squeeze the great bulk of its operating needs from its own citizens.

Taxation. It is absolutely inevitable. In this regard it is usually mentioned in the same breath as death, but the truth may be that taxation is even more inevitable than death. Some learned scientists have estimated that future generations of men may be able to postpone death and live for centuries. But there is no possibility—absolutely none—that our descendants will invent a universal escape from taxation. As a matter of fact, the historical record suggests that the taxation of the future will probably be even heavier and more painful than what we know today. The bigger and more complex a nation gets, the bigger each citizen's tax bite gets. There is no known way around this law. A corollary law is that as taxation grows heavier, the administration of the tax grows inexorably more confused and corrupt. We may have cause to be thankful that we are living now, not in the 25th Century.

Money equals work, more or less. Boiled down to its essentials, taxation is a means by which each citizen is made to contribute his share of work to the operation and improvement of his society. In fact, until money came into wide use, most taxes were paid directly in the form of work. A farmer would be required, either by formal government edict or by social pressure from his neighbors, to quit his own field for a while and help build a defense wall or an irrigation canal for the community. Tax historians are fond of pointing out that human societies are not unique in this respect. Beavers, bees, ants and other busy and social creatures share work in much the same way. The difference is that beavers, bees and ants don't mind doing it.

The average taxpaying bee, so I'm told, spends most of his days working for the hive rather than himself. He has no personal bank account and he doesn't even have his own sex life. The tax rate he pays, if it can be translated into terms of money, must be something like 95%. To the average American, who spends a third of his adult life working to pay taxes, it may be comforting to know that there are creatures on earth in worse shape than he.

Yet, to say "worse" is to commit the philosophical error of reading human feelings into a nonhuman society.

Worker bees appear to pay their enormous taxes quite willingly. The few I've known personally have looked somewhat gloomy, but not actively dissatisfied. Humans, by contrast, almost never pay taxes willingly. Historically, whenever a tax rate has risen higher than about 10% of income, the government levying the tax has had to maintain a large police force to insure more than token compliance.

Informal taxes, in the form of goods as well as work, probably came into existence when the first nomadic bands of hunters organized themselves into tribes before the dawn of written history. It is probable that the tribal citizens were assessed to provide the chief's food and clothing, the tribe's military hardware and other governmental needs. It is equally probable that the citizens grumbled.

The ancient Egyptians, some 3,000 years ago, were the first to mention taxes in writing. King Ramses II once had a kind of financial prayer inscribed on a stone tablet, and in this prayer he asked his god to accept various tax-like tributes that appear to have been gathered by means of a special assessment on the citizens.

As far as we can tell, those early Egyptian taxes were collected with a minimum of paper work. (The invention of paper is said to have been good for humanity, but it has had its disadvantages.) Tax collectors, representing the king or the priesthood, simply roamed about the country demanding goods or services. A potter, for example, might be asked to contribute a vase or two. The value of what he contributed probably had little to do with his income, though it is conceivable, even likely, that he would plead poverty in trying to talk the collectors down to one vase instead of two. At any rate, he filled out no Form 1040. The tax bite gouged out of him depended on his stubbornness in arguing with the collectors, on their determination to collect (they may have operated on a commission basis, or may have had a quota system as we in IRS have today) and probably on the taxpayer's willingness to pay a bribe. No tax law in modern history has ever been administered without large-scale bribery, and there is no good reason to guess ancient Egyptian TPs and revenue agents were any more honest than modern Americans or Europeans.

That ancient system might be labeled the casual or negotiated tax. If a citizen could hide from the collectors, he paid nothing. If they found him, he paid something, but not according to any fixed scale or formalized set of percentages. In its way that may have been the world's most manageable tax law. It might even have been fun. It required little record-keeping. And since those who paid the lowest taxes probably kept the fact to themselves, there may not have been much grumbling about inequities.

By the time of Greece's golden age, the casual tax was giving way rapidly to more formalized and more annoying concepts. Solon introduced the idea of a net-wealth tax, under which each citizen was supposed to pay according to how much property he owned. Nausinicus introduced a nongraduated income tax. According to Plutarch, the citizens paid their taxes without much grumbling, probably because the rates were basically low and the richest citizens could always secure lower rates by bribery. Plutarch claims that when Pericles asked the Athenian Assembly whether he should reduce governmental spending and cut taxes, the citizens said no, he should go on spending as he saw fit. If that is true, it was one of the few instances in history in which a people actually voted against an offered tax cut.

Frankly, as a revenue agent I find the story highly unlikely. Plutarch was misled somehow. He may have picked up the story by reading some document, or hearing some word-of-mouth legend originated by one of Pericles' tax officials—a Greek equivalent, perhaps, of our Commissioner of Internal Revenue. Down through history, tax officials have always tried to maintain the fiction that people really like to pay taxes. Like dentists, they keep saying it doesn't hurt. Nobody ever believes this fiction, but it is an honored tradition of the tax-collecting business and it still lives strongly today. Our modern commissioners of Internal Revenue religiously repeat the assertion that "97% of Americans pay their taxes voluntarily." This is nonsense, of course.

The ancient Romans tried a casual kind of nongraduated income tax, but found it too hard to administer. Despite Cicero's assertion that Romans were honest, nobody wanted to say what his real income was. Since all transactions were in goods, services or cash, Roman revenue agents had no convenient way to find out how badly a citizen was lying, though they could usually assume he was. Moreover, there seems to have been a good deal of corruption in the government bureaus, and the richest taxpayers probably ended up paying the least tax.

The Romans abandoned that idea and turned to others. They paid special and cynical attention to taxes that could be collected easily, taxes that did not depend on the honesty of the taxpayer. One such tax was levied on the gross receipts of public auctions. Since an auction was conducted out in the open where a revenue agent could stand around with the Roman equivalent of a little black notebook, there was no need to ask the taxpayer how much money he took in. Another tax, similar in general philosophy, was levied on prostitutes. The prostitute was not asked to state her annual income, nor offered any other chance to lie. Instead, she paid a flat tax based on the size of her fee for a single act of service. A revenue agent could easily determine the fee by posing as, or becoming, a client.

Still another Roman tax, based on this same idea of easy administration in a dishonest world, was a kind of levy that might be called a wealth-clue tax. It was similar to the Greeks' net-wealth tax in that each citizen paid according to the amount of property he ostensibly owned. But the Romans, perhaps more cynical than the Greeks, figured there was no sense trying to find out what a taxpayer's real wealth was, since wealth could be hidden. Instead, Roman revenue men guessed at each TP's wealth by looking at certain visible clues, such as the number of slaves or horses he owned. He paid a fixed annual tax for each slave and each horse that he was unable to hide.

This wealth-clue idea became common in Europe during the Middle Ages. In England and Ireland, for example, families were taxed according to the number of windows in their houses, and at other times the number of hearths or chimneys. These taxes had an effect on architecture, particularly in Ireland where windowless houses were common until the 18th Century.

Early European attempts at an income tax were not successful. In fact they were disastrous. Florence replaced a property tax with an income tax in the middle of the 15th Century, but it degenerated into a welter of confusion, corruption, wholesale bribery, extortion, murder and other nasty phenomena. The tax disappeared when Florence ceased to be a democracy in the 16th Century. The French were next to try an income tax, early in the 18th

Century. It was so badly administered that some historians list it among the main dissatisfactions that led to the French Revolution.

Like our present income tax, French prerevolution taxes fell most heavily on what we today would call the middle class. Nobles, clergymen, government administrators and other privileged folk escaped most taxes handily, either through bribery or personal influence, or through the simple expedient of passing special tax-preference laws. Most of the tax money was gouged out of peasants, farmers and small landowners, the so-called Third Estate. Even the French nobility and clergy, though evidently blind to many other truths of their time, realized there was no future in trying to squeeze a lot of tax money out of a poor man. Thus the most harshly squeezed were the more successful members of the Third Estate. They were subject to all kinds of taxes, of which the most hated was the income tax.

There was no government bureau quite analogous to our beloved IRS. Instead, the French government sold tax-collecting privileges to an odd group of speculators called *fermiers généraux*. These were wealthy men who—to state the case simply—advanced money to the government. Each was then licensed to go out and collect the money from the citizens of his district. If he could collect more than he had advanced, the excess was his to keep.

Some *fermiers généraux* were fair and sympathetic to the taxpayers, but others weren't. They hired gangs of toughs to do the assessing and collecting. Compared to them, the modern American revenue man—a fellow like me, for instance—is ridiculously gentle, even lovable. Some French collection gangs, working on a commission basis, used tax-extraction methods of the most brutal sort. Taxpayers were routinely beaten or tortured to make them reveal where they had hidden their money. A man's entire store of movable goods might be confiscated: His horse would be loaded with his furniture and his pots and pans; his cow would be tied behind his horse; and the two would be led away, leaving him effectively bankrupt. Taxpayers caught cheating were sometimes hung.

The French income tax was promptly guillotined by the revolutionaries when they seized power. The next nation to try the idea was England, in 1799.

The British set three precedents that have been honored since by nearly every other nation in organizing an income tax. First, the tax was graduated (from about 0.8% to a top rate of 10%), with the highest rates charged to upper-middle citizens. In this sense, the British tax of 1799 was the first modern income tax.

Second, the new tax was started in wartime (the Napoleonic Wars) and was billed to the people as a temporary, emergency measure that would be repealed when the crisis was over. It was repealed and reenacted several times over the next 40-odd years, but the essential fact is that it never really died as the politicians promised. It remained in effect through war and peace, crisis or no crisis. It is still in effect today, more than 170 years later. This has been the history of all major nations' income taxes, including ours. They were all supposed to be temporary.

The third precedent set by those 18th-Century Englishmen was that their income tax was stunningly complicated. The original law twisted and backtracked and huffed and puffed its way through 152 barely intelligible pages. And almost immediately, of course, it began to get worse as exceptions and loopholes were written in. At least two enterprising publishers of the period quickly printed Lasser-like pamphlets to explain the tax to the baffled TPs.

The British people profoundly hated the graduated income tax, as have all people ever since. Dozens of pamphlets denouncing it sprang from the presses. The British were already paying a number of other taxes—on windows, horses, land, servants—and the income tax on top of those felt like a crushing burden. Tax collectors in London and elsewhere were pelted with stones and rotten fruit, while pamphleteers pelted them with words such as "merciless mercenaries" and "brutes." The tax was hated so violently that when it was repealed for a time after the British victory at Waterloo, Parliament ordered all records pertaining to it destroyed. But it sprang to life again, like some science-fiction monster whose appalled creator can't kill it.

One thing that particularly angered those early income-taxpayers was the government's wide use of freelance informers. We use and pay informers today at IRS (see Chapter 11), but we don't actively recruit them and we keep quiet about them. The British government, however, advertised loudly that it would be pleased to receive information about tax cheats and would pay squealers handsomely. The poet and essayist Robert Southey, a keen observer of the period, likened the tax-collection mechanism to the Spanish Inquisition. "This species of espionage has . . . become a regular trade," he wrote bitterly. "A fellow . . . informs the tax commissioners that certain persons have given in a false account . . . an offense for which the tax is trebled, and half the surplus given to the informer." (The most we pay an informer today is 10%.)

Southey also felt the tax laws could have been simpler. "The laws are in some instances so perplexing," he wrote, "and in others so vexatious, that matter for prosecution is never wanting." Lucky Southey. He never saw the tax monstrosities that were to be erected in the 20th Century.

Meanwhile a new nation called the United States had come into being across the Atlantic. It had been born partly because its people objected to British taxation—in fact, to taxation of any kind—and this strong emotion was to play a key role in many acts and scenes of its subsequent history. Its brave and prickly people were to resist a permanent income tax for the first 137 years of the nation's life.

The Continental Congress had a lot of problems over taxes. The Articles of Confederation talked about federal revenue-raising in a vague way, but in practice most federal money came from the separate states, which taxed their citizens in a casual fashion and were supposed to turn some of the cash in to the Congress. Often, one state or another would fail to come up with the cash. People would grumble at the delinquent state, but wouldn't go much beyond that, for taxation was an explosive subject in those days. Prod it too hard, and people would blow up.

Many states and communities had land, wealth-clue and other taxes on their books, but if the citizens didn't feel like paying, in many cases they simply didn't pay. According to some early accounts in Connecticut, for example, the major share of the tax burden was apparently inherited by the meek. A tax collector would go up to a farmer and say, "You owe a tax on that horse."

"What horse?" the farmer would say.

"Why, that one over there."

"I don't see any horse. Do you see a horse, boys?"

The farmer's three or four burly sons would say no, they didn't see a horse either.

The collector would nod politely and say, "Right, no horse. See you next year."

Through its first century of existence, the U.S. federal government got the bulk of its revenues from customs duties and internal excise taxes (one of which led to the Whiskey Rebellion of 1791), and from sales of land in the Midwest and West. The first federal man to make noises about an income tax was Alexander Dallas, Treasury Secretary under President Madison. He committed this indiscretion during the War of 1812. Though he carefully used the word "temporary" in talking about the tax, Congress told him rather rudely to keep his mad thoughts to himself. The war ended, and the subject was not brought up seriously again until the Civil War.

That war brought on the first U.S. income tax, which went into effect in 1862. It was called an "income duty." The rates ranged from 3% to 5%. It was one of history's few examples of an income tax which, billed as temporary, stayed temporary. It was enthusiastically killed in 1871.

During its decade of life the income duty raised some $376 million in revenue, roughly 0.02% of the amount we collected in the single year 1971. The nation wasn't very big in those days. Nor was there any easy way to dig the duty out of citizens who didn't feel dutiful. In the income tax's best year, 1866, the government collected more than twice as much money from customs duties and three times as much from internal excises.

One of the main reasons for killing the income tax was the simple fact that it didn't work right. Though it was amended six times, it only seemed to get more confusing and self-contradictory each time. It only made people mad. Its inefficiency was a major argument against income taxation for the next several decades.

Among the few people who seem to have derived any contentment from the Civil War income tax was Mark Twain. In 1864 he paid a tax of $36.82, plus a $3.12 fine for late filing. He remarked happily that the tax made him feel "important"; the cold and distant government was at last paying attention to him. Many citizens of a less expansive nature, however, felt they could get along without this cozy feeling that somebody in Washington cared. Nonpayment of the tax filled them with an equally pleasant warmth.

The nation's next skirmish with an income tax began in the early 1890s. (By this time almost every other major nation had such a tax.) President Cleveland had been elected partly by presenting himself as the poor man's friend. One plank of his platform held that tariffs should be used for revenue-raising purposes only, rather than as trade barriers to protect domestic industries. Many poor and middle-income Americans agreed. They saw tariffs as mechanisms to keep prices artificially high, thus fattening the rich at the expense of the nonrich. Cleveland, once elected, kept his promises and cut tariffs substantially. This left him embarrassingly short of revenue in a rapidly growing nation that needed ever more federal services. And so, renewing his campaign talk about redistributing wealth to the poor, he proposed an income tax.

His proposal was modest—it called for a tax that would nip a uniform 2% from all incomes over $4,000. But he might as well have asked for 90%. The influential rich, along with their many friends in Congress, reacted with outrage and horror. "Socialism, communism and devilism!" roared Senator John Sherman, the father of the Sherman Antitrust Act. Another senator howled: "If we pass this bill, free enterprise dies on this spot! We shall tax the hard-working and the successful while letting the lazy and improvident go." In the House, a congressman called the tax "odious" and "unutterably distasteful both in its moral and material aspects." He predicted: "The imposition of this tax will corrupt the people. It will bring in its train the spy and the informer. It will necessitate a swarm of officials with inquisitorial powers. . . ."

His prediction was correct on all three counts, especially the last. But the prediction did not come true immediately, for President Cleveland's income tax never went into effect. It was enacted into law in 1894, but before the first income-tax return could be printed, the Supreme Court shot the new tax down. A federal income tax, said the court, was clearly unconstitutional. (This same objection had been raised over the Civil War income tax, but the nation had needed the money so badly back then that the objectors were hooted down as unpatriotic, quibbling nitpickers.) The Constitution said all federal "direct taxes" had to be apportioned among the states on the basis of population, and that was the Supreme Court's stated reason for killing the 1894 income-tax law. But the court's action also stemmed from the fact that most of the justices simply didn't like the idea of taxing income.

"This is class legislation," grumbled Justice Field. Because the law would tax the rich more than the poor—would tax success, in other words—he held it to be discriminatory and unfair. Such legislation, he said, "leads inevitably to oppression and abuses and to general unrest and disturbances in society." He grumpily likened the tax to an early British one in which Protestants paid one rate, Catholics twice that much, Jews still more.

And so the nation enjoyed two more blissful decades without a federal income tax. Virginia tried a state income tax in 1909 and 1910, but it was a miserable failure. The state collected only a little over $100,000 in two years' time. In nearly a third of its counties, it collected nothing at all; the hardy citizens simply didn't want to pay the tax, and the state found no effective way to make them do it. No sane revenue agent wanted to go into the rural counties and argue with shotguns. A few apparently insane agents tried it, and at least one was never seen or heard of again.

Despite the obvious difficulties, Congress revived the hated question of a federal income tax in 1909. Desperate for revenue and worried about the possibility of war in Europe, Congress proposed amending the Constitution so as to make such a tax legal. Most congressmen were thinking in terms of a temporary income tax that could be shut off when the financial emergency was over, perhaps to be turned on again like a faucet whenever other emergencies arose in the future. But before either a temporary or permanent income tax could go into effect, Step One was to doctor that accommodating document, the Constitution.

The outcry against the idea was predictably loud and emotional, but by early 1913 two-thirds of the states had ratified the 16th Amendment, and it became the law of the land. The federal government was now allowed to tax "all income, from whatever source derived."

The first income-tax law glued together by Congress later that year was long and confusing, a fearful harbinger of complexities to come. Rep. Cordell Hull, its author, had to explain it to Congress. Boiled down to its essentials, it provided for a normal tax of 1% on incomes of $3,000 to $20,000 (the starting point was $4,000 for a married taxpayer), with a modest surtax on incomes above that level. The highest surtax was 6%, on incomes over $500,000. There was also a 1% tax on corporate income. To us in the

1970s that sounds like heaven, but the taxable citizens of 1913 felt they had been dealt a low blow. Of course, there were only a few million such citizens, for the incomes of most Americans back then were below the $4,000 cutoff point, and this was precisely what troubled the taxable minority. They felt they had been unjustly singled out for persecution. The *New York Times,* which in those days tended to side with the wealthy in most arguments, editorialized on April 12, 1913, that the new tax had "transferred the burdens of the many to the shoulders of the few." In Wall Street there were bitter complaints that the tax was a Communist plot, the first step in some great, sinister plan for siphoning money away from the rich and destroying capitalism. (Karl Marx had in fact suggested years before that a graduated income tax might be used for just this purpose.) Continuing its complaints, the *Times* grumbled that the new law "will tax the honest and allow the dishonest to escape." Moreover, grumped the *Times,* the new law was so complicated that it discriminated unjustly against people who didn't happen to be good at mathematics. Not taken in by political promises that the tax was temporary, the *Times* pessimistically forecast that the rates would eventually double (to a basic 2%, that is; an interesting example of how to be resoundingly right and ridiculously wrong at the same time).

By 1921 the tax was not only politically acknowledged and popularly assumed to be permanent, but was growing like some gigantic, incurable cancer. The 1921 first-bracket rate was 4% on incomes over $4,000, and the top rate was 73% on incomes above $1 million. By 1944 the tax had reached its gaudy climax: 23% on incomes over $2,000, up to 94% on incomes above $200,000. By this time it had become a mass tax. With wages rising dramatically and the tax cutoff point dropping, millions of new TPs were being sucked into the great taxation machine.

The tax has subsided a little since the 1940s, but only a little and only on paper. Because of inflation, middle-income U.S. citizens today pay a bigger share of their income in taxes than ever before in the history of the country or, as far as I know, of the world.

To see how this painful effect has been quietly operating over the years, suppose for simplicity that the effective tax rate is 20% on a $10,000 annual income and twice that, or 40%, on a $20,000 income. For further simplicity, suppose that these rates have remained unchanged for 30 years.

All right. Thirty years ago a $10,000 income put a family solidly in a prosperous stratum of the middle class, and the family gave IRS 20% of its income. Today it takes an income of $20,000 to buy what that $10,000 income did 30 years ago. And yet, earning the same real income, the family pays twice as much tax.

So whenever a politician or a tax commissioner tries to soothe you by claiming income taxes were once higher than they are today, don't believe it. It is a paper illusion. We stand today at an historic high.

For fun, let's look at some IRS statistics going back to the birth of the income tax. (Perhaps "fun" is the wrong word. If you cry easily, I sympathetically suggest that you skip the next few paragraphs.) In 1914, IRS collected $380 million in total taxes, including the newborn income tax. Dividing that figure by the total population, this worked out to a minuscule and charming $3.88 per capita.

In 1920, a bare six years later, total tax collections were something like $5.5 billion. The per-capita figure was up to $50.81—a six-year increase so enormous and shocking that the first appreciable wave of tax avoiders began flowing to Europe.

A 20-year slump in collections followed. Income-tax rates were reduced in the 1920s, as were certain other taxes; and in the 1930s income itself was reduced by a painful and protracted depression. The low year was 1932. Total collections that year were about $1.5 billion, and the per-capita figure was down to a modest $12.48. In that dismal year only some 3.5 million people, in a population of 125 million, had enough income to be taxed.

From then on, it was uphill most of the way. Collections per capita were $40.57 in 1940; $256.44 in 1950; $507.98 in 1960; and $960.67 in 1970.

Total collections in 1970 were $196 billion. That astounding figure is very nearly impossible to hold in the mind. Its colossal size can be visualized vaguely by various kinds of "if" games, but even they are hardly equal to the task. If you distributed all that money around the world, every man, woman and child on the planet would get about 50 bucks. If a benevolent IRS gave you permission to take the money in the form of dollar bills, and if you managed to stagger home with $100,000 an hour, you would reach the end of your life quite rich and with an aching back—but without having made an appreciable dent in the mountainous pile. To get all of it you would have to work eight hours a day, 365 days a year, for about 600 years. But if the $196 billion were put in savings banks while you were struggling to carry it away, and if it drew simple annual interest at 5%, you would have to multiply your efforts tenfold just to keep up with the interest, which would be about a million dollars an hour. And if . . .

But enough of this foolishness. Let's content ourselves

by saying $196 billion is more money than can be imagined.

IRS has some 69,000 employees today to collect these colossal loads of money. Back in 1914 it had 3,972. A quick reading of the statistics would seem to indicate that contrary to Parkinson's laws, the small, cozy organization of 1914 didn't do its work as efficiently as the huge mob we've got today. In 1914 it cost IRS $1.52 to collect each $100 of taxes, while in 1970 it cost only 45¢. Revenue commissioners are fond of quoting these statistics to show what a good job they're doing, but the fact is that this apparent increase in efficiency results mainly from higher tax rates. It takes nearly as much work to squeeze $100 out of a given TP as to squeeze out $1,000. The revenue agents of 1914 were at a disadvantage in the efficiency game. For every ounce of squeeze, they got less juice. In IRS today we enjoy the advantages of a bigger-volume business.

It cost IRS $981 million—very nearly a billion dollars —to collect the taxes in 1971. This outlay was more than the total collections in 1915 and 1916 put together. Somehow, contemplating figures like these, I get an uncomfortable feeling that things are getting out of hand. There has never before been a nation that *spent* a billion dollars collecting its taxes.

Part of the reason for this staggering cost is the sheer complexity of the nation, of its citizens' affairs, and of the tax laws themselves. A revenue agent like me can spend days going over a taxpayer's returns, only to find in the end, perhaps, that the TP owes nothing—or, worse, that IRS owes the man a refund. The theory behind this is that by buzzing one TP I keep ten others honest. Perhaps. Yet it does seem to me that ways could be found to simplify this increasingly tangled mess.

The history of the laws since 1913 has been one of complexity inexorably compounded. Congress has continually tinkered with the laws in response to various pressures, sometimes from the middle masses, most often from the wealthy. IRS itself writes hundreds of new administrative rules every year. The courts sometimes uphold the laws and rules and sometimes don't. And IRS sometimes says it will go along with court decisions and sometimes says it won't—and sometimes does what it says and sometimes doesn't. Even if a taxpayer could read all the millions of written words that supposedly represent this restless sea of law at any given moment, he still would not know where he stood.

The word "loophole," as applied to the tax laws, first came into use in the 1930s. But people were complaining about the phenomenon as far back as 1915. A congressman was trying to explain to a newspaper reporter why the original 1913 law, not simple to begin with, was steadily and rapidly growing more complicated. He outlined the process like this: "I write a law. You drill a hole in it. I plug the hole. You drill a hole in my plug."

And thus it has continued to the present day.

PART II

THE PEOPLE UNDER, AROUND, OVER AND THROUGH THE TAX

Wherein we contemplate the games played by evaders, avoiders, invaders and raiders.

Chapter 6

THE
BACKWARD-GRADUATED
TAX

My group chief called me into his office one morning to talk about a case that puzzled him. A married taxpayer with a name something like Bunker had taken advantage of his apparent poverty and filed the simplest of all possible tax returns, the one-page 1040. He had stated his adjusted gross income for the year as slightly over $2,000. In the space that asked for his occupation he had written, "Poet." No tax had been withheld from his income during the year, and he had paid it in full with his return: a grand total of $58.

One thing that puzzled my chief was the manner of payment. Somebody up at the district office had noticed it, had been similarly puzzled and had routed the return to our field office with a request that we look into it. Bunker, the poverty-stricken poet, had paid his tax with a machine-written check.

Most married couples with incomes in the $2,000 range don't even have bank accounts. They pay their taxes, if any, with money orders or postage stamps or plain cash. In rural areas, some even try to pay with goods and services. They will show up at a field office with old cars or bundles of old clothes or bags of tomatoes they've grown in their backyards, or they'll offer to wash the office windows in lieu of tax. But here was this Bunker, paying with a machine-written check of the kind that you commonly associate with big corporations or the wealthiest individuals.

It was conceivable that Bunker and his wife had rich parents in whose home they lived and off whom they sponged, enjoying the privileges of wealth while earning only a small taxable income. But my chief wanted me to look into the case anyway. He was curious.

Bunker, on the phone, turned out to be a prickly and somewhat arrogant fellow. He had one of those bored, pseudo-British voices that certain intellectuals affect. He called me "my dear Mr. Revenue." He began by saying he didn't have time to waste with what he called "accountant types," in which category he evidently included me. I pointed out, very courteously of course, that he was obliged by law to waste whatever time I wanted him to waste. He finally said all right, he'd talk to me, but he wasn't going to come to my office. I would have to come to him. Since I always jump at a chance to get out of the office, I made a brief show of reluctance and then set a date.

His home was a huge English Tudor mansion. I parked my four-year-old Ford next to a brand-new Maserati in the driveway and was shown through the house by a maid. Bunker was sitting by a swimming pool in the back. He was a man of perhaps 35, in swimming trunks and dark glasses. He was drinking a highball. He didn't offer me one. I wouldn't have accepted, but I would have appreciated a cup of coffee.

"Let's get this over with fast," he said. "I don't like business and I don't want my life cluttered up with tax forms and accountants. I've deliberately made my life simple. I see that troubles the bureaucratic mind. You wonder how I can be wealthy but only pay a fifty-dollar tax."

He proceeded to explain. He had inherited a generous block of stock from his father years ago. After all the applicable taxes were paid, he had ended up with $13 million. He had put the entire amount into municipal bonds. At an average tax-free yield of 4%, these brought him an income of somewhat more than $500,000 a year. Not only was this income untaxable, he wasn't even obliged to declare it. To occupy his time, he said, he had begun writing poetry and short stories last year for small literary magazines. The $2,000 he had earned was his only taxable income.

I went away feeling gloomy. A revenue agent is required to uphold the law, but he isn't required to like it. I've always felt—and after leaving Bunker felt more acutely than ever—that there is something wrong with an income tax that doesn't tax all incomes alike, and particularly with one that often taxes the rich less than the poor. An ordinary wage or salary earner produces income with his own brain and backbone, and that income is fully taxed. A man like Bunker, making little or no productive contribution to society, gets a free ride.

There are reasons for exempting certain types of bond interest from taxation. In my opinion they aren't good reasons, but all right, let's not argue the point here. Let's even grant the reasons are sound. What bothers me is the *effect* of such a setup. The effect is to make the income tax regressive, to graduate it backward so that the dice are loaded in favor of the wealthy.

In the pious theory of income taxation, a progressive tax is supposed to encourage capital accumulation by those who don't yet have much capital. Those in the lower- and middle-income strata should be able to gather their nest eggs with relative ease. The gathering process should get progressively tougher as you climb up the strata, for the assumption is that the wealthy, already possessing large amounts of capital, need no special help from the government in gathering more.

Arrangements such as the tax-free bond deal—and it is only one of many—do just the opposite. The average working man or middle-class salary earner doesn't buy municipal bonds. Even if he wanted to, he could buy only a few and could enjoy only a minor amount of tax-free income. Since his main income is taxed at stiff rates, he finds it grindingly difficult to accumulate any capital at all except perhaps a partial equity in a house, a small savings account and a few mutual-fund shares. Thus the existence of nontaxable bond interest is no favor to him. Bonds are bought by those who *already have* capital, by those who don't need the favor of tax exemption.

The day after I audited Bunker, I was still mad. I went out to audit the tax return of a stationery-store owner in a small suburban town. This taxpayer—he had a German name something like Klotz—was exactly the kind of stomped-upon citizen I had been feeling sorry for. He was in his middle fifties. He had worked hard all his life, and all he had to show for it was a little house somewhere, a grubby little store and not even enough savings to pay his tax bill. His taxes for the year had amounted to more than $2,000, and he had had to borrow to pay the last installment. The economic and tax environment in which he was forced to live had made it impossible for him to gather capital.

I noticed something interesting about his return. His mother was living in his home, but since she had earned more than $600 during the year he hadn't been able to claim her as an exemption.

I asked how much she had earned. He said $800 or so.

"She's over sixty-five?" I asked.

"Seventy-two," he said.

The law said that if you were that old you didn't have to file any tax return at all unless your income was over $1,200. I asked Klotz if his mother had in fact filed a return, and he said no.

"How did she earn this eight hundred?" I asked.

"Babysitting, mainly. Seamstress work now and then. Odd jobs like that."

"Who keeps the records of her income?"

"She does. She jots it down in a little book and gives me the total at the end of the year."

I could see my questions had Klotz worried. I froze my face into an expression of cold disapproval, what one of my chiefs used to call the Bureaucratic Look, very useful for intimidating taxpayers. I said, "Well, now listen, Mr. Klotz. Around IRS we don't trust the memories of elderly ladies. If this was an eight-hundred-dollar expense deduction you were claiming, do you suppose I'd accept your mother's word for it? You can bet your shirt I wouldn't. I'd disallow at least half of it unless you could come up with documentary evidence. So I'm going to be consistent. If your mother can't prove she made eight hundred dollars, I'm going to guess she only made five hundred and ninety-nine. That gives you a new exemption, and it means you've paid about a hundred and fifty bucks too much tax."

When I left, Klotz looked dazed. The $150 refund he was going to get wouldn't lift him into the class of the great capital gatherers, but at least it might help him a little. It was a token of my disgust with the system. The rest of that day, I felt better.

But the next day I audited another wealthy fellow whose major income was in the form of long-term capital gains, taxed in that year at the top rate of 25%. My euphoria vanished.

The capital-gains tax is another case of backward graduation. As the law defines it, a capital gain is a profit you make by selling anything you own—a share of stock, a house, a cow, a collection of postage stamps, a wad of foreign currency. Technically, the thing you sell is supposed to be outside your regular trade or business; otherwise the profit is considered ordinary income rather than a capital gain. That is, if you're a professional dealer in rare coins, the profits you make in the course of buying and selling coins are plain income; but if you aren't a coin dealer, the profits from the same transactions would be capital gains. There are exceptions to this rule—loopholes within loopholes—but let's not make this discussion any more complicated than it need be. Let's look at the basic idea of the capital-gains tax.

The basic idea is a honey, provided you're rich. If your gain is long-term—meaning that you owned the property at least six months before selling it—you are taxed on only half of it. To put it another way, you pay only half the tax rate you would pay if this were plain earned income.

A capital gain is money earned by money. Why is this kind of income favored over money earned by the sweat of a man's brow? The rationale is that the capital-gains tax is supposed to encourage capital accumulation. Rich folks repeatedly assure Congress that if this special tax preference were repealed, the result would be a national economic collapse. Corporations wouldn't be able to sell enough stock to raise cash for operations and expansion; people's jobs would disappear; a horrible depression would seize the country, and we'd all go down the drain. I strongly doubt this, but all right, let's even grant that it is true. If it is to be national policy to encourage capital accumulation, why not spread some of the largesse down to us poor old working folks? Why not invent a different kind of tax preference (I can think of several dozen possible approaches) that would help *everybody* gather capital, instead of merely making the rich richer?

For that is what the present capital-gains tax does: It distinctly and almost immorally favors the rich. To score any capital gain, obviously, you must have capital to begin with. To score a long-term gain, you must be in the comfortable position of owning capital you don't need to touch for at least half a year. To score capital gains in appreciable amounts—that is, to get more than a token benefit from the preference—*you must already be rich.*

Down here among us middle-income folks, the capital-gains preference is like Tantalus's water, which eternally receded from his parched lips. Once in a while we get a small taste of it, just enough to make us want more; we sell a few shares of stock, maybe, or we angle ourselves into some minor capital-gains deal in a profit-sharing plan. Once in a great while we might reap a fair-sized gain by selling a house. But the great bulk of our income in a typical year is earned by our own brain and muscle, not by our money. Since brain-and-muscle income is fully taxed, we have but little chance to accumulate the kind of capital that can earn meaningful amounts of half-taxed money. We must spend most or all (in some cases more than all) of our income for current living expenses and taxes.

A 1972 study by the Brookings Institution in Washington, D.C., illustrated this fact starkly. Brookings approached IRS and asked for computer tapes representing a large bundle of actual tax returns from all income levels. The tapes contained all the data that would appear on a return except the taxpayer's identity. The Revenue Service was pleased to help Brookings this way because, as I've said, we are not required to love the law we are employed to enforce. Many revenue people, from lowly agents like myself up to some of the highest officials, would like very much to see the tax laws made simpler and more equitable. So IRS handed over the tapes, and Brookings subjected them to a computerized statistical analysis.

One part of the study dealt with capital gains. Brookings sought to find out how much money is saved by taxpayers in various income levels through the capital-gains preference. It turned out as expected. The average taxpayer with an annual income of $500,000 to a million dollars in an average year saves $165,000 in taxes by paying the capital-gains rates instead of the full rates. The average taxpayer in the $20,000-to-$25,000 bracket saves a paltry $120. And the fellow in the $5,000-to-$10,000 range saves eight bucks.

I once audited a man who thought he had an answer to this problem. He was an engineer with a salary of about $15,000 and with a wife and two kids to support. Because his economic situation was almost identical to my own, I listened to him with great sympathy. I found him likable and persuasive. I wished I could help him.

His approach was a novel one. The only capital he had in the world was a small savings account. He had about $4,000 in it, as I recall, and during the tax year this money had earned him some $200 in interest. In figuring out his taxes, he had treated the interest as a capital gain.

The law says explicitly that bank interest is income, not a capital gain. I explained this to him gently.

"I know what the law says," he replied, "but the law is crazy. That savings account is capital, right? When the bank credits interest to it and I leave the interest sitting in the account, the interest becomes capital too, doesn't it? I gain capital through interest. So why isn't interest considered a capital gain?"

I had never thought of this before. I shrugged. "I don't know why," I said. "All I know is, it's the law."

This was a cowardly answer, of course. It was the Civil Service Waltz: "I don't make the rules; I just do what I'm told." I was instantly ashamed of ducking his question that way, and to soothe my conscience I encouraged him to tell me more about his theory.

He made sense. He pointed out what I had long ago noticed on my own—that the capital-gains preference loads the dice in favor of those who are already rich. Millions of lower- and middle-income taxpayers look to savings accounts as their main route of capital accumulation, in many cases their only feasible route. A man struggling to feed his family may not feel he can trust his tiny wad of capital to the stock market. The risks there are too high for him. More than anything else, he needs safety for his money. He also needs liquidity—the assurance that he can get to his cash fast in an emergency—and this keeps him out of real-estate speculation and other possible investments. He is left with bank savings as his only hope. And of all the common modes of investment, bank savings are the only type that offer no possibility of capital-gains treatment.

Any accountant will tell you, of course, that there are reasons for treating interest as plain income. Lawmakers have found it necessary to make distinctions between the growth of capital itself and the money earned *by* capital. If you invest your money in an apartment building and collect rent, the rent is income. If you sell the building at a profit, the profit is a capital gain. Bank interest is considered to be earned in the same sense that apartment rent is earned, and therefore is called income. But this distinction is so fine that it must be called arbitrary. It could be argued just as facilely that interest is a gain in capital.

The engineer argued facilely. When he had finished I said, "I agree with everything you say. But I've still got to assess you for the extra tax. It's your privilege to appeal if you want, but I warn you, you won't get anywhere."

The engineer was angry. "I'll appeal!" he shouted.

But the next day he phoned me and said sorrowfully that he had cooled off and changed his mind. The amount of tax money involved—30 bucks or so—was too small to warrant the expense and aggravation. He was giving up.

This is another thing that strikes me as unfair about our tax system. If a rich taxpayer gets into an argument with me about half a million dollars in taxes, it's worth his while to fight a good fight. He can hire lawyers and accountants to fight it for him, and the U.S. government will help him defray the cost, for their fees are tax-deductible. But the little guy generally has no other practical choice but to knuckle under and do what I say. Sure, we've got an internal appeals system at IRS and even a special small-claims tax court where a taxpayer can argue his own case without hiring lawyers. But the ordinary low- to middle-income man can't afford to take the time off from work. Even if he could, he may figure that the 30 or a hundred bucks he is arguing about won't pay him for the stomach ulcers and headaches he'll get out of the argument. Indeed, the disputed amount—if he wins—may not even pay his travel expenses to the IRS offices and the court. We collect millions of small checks from small taxpayers this way. It is very easy for a revenue agent to bully a small taxpayer, forcing him to accept a decision that the taxpayer could dispute if only he had the means. I remember once auditing an assembly-plant worker who claimed his house had been damaged in a storm. His story was that the storm had torn off some roof shingles, water had leaked into an upstairs bedroom, and it had cost him some $300 to repair the damage. Subtracting $100 from this figure, as the law requires, he was claiming a casualty deduction of about $200.

I am not proud to say this, but I was in no mood to listen to this story at the time. I was behind on my quota. We didn't have a formal quota system in my office; no agent was required to bring in a certain amount of money per week or month. But we did have an informal system, a definite sense of pressure to "produce." The group chief had cleverly instilled a sense of competition among the agents. If any agent fell below the general norm in the number of cases he closed or the amount of money he brought in, the chief would call that agent in and wonder aloud whether he really had what it took to do this kind of work. And I hadn't been doing well for a number of weeks. By sheer bad luck, I had run into a long string of prickly taxpayers, all rich, all surrounded by lawyers and tax experts. I had closed few cases and brought in little money. And so I was not kind to the assembly-plant man. I disallowed his $200 casualty loss. I told him such a loss is deductible only when it demonstrably results from some sudden, violent, destructive force. The storm he was talking about hadn't been violent enough to make the newspapers; it was just a summer thunderstorm. Moreover, I pointed out, his house was old and it could be assumed the roof had been slowly deteriorating for years. The shingles might have come off at any time. You can't make a casualty deduction out of slow deterioration.

He argued. His case was good. If he had had the time and the money and the gumption, he might easily have won it on appeal. But it was lamentably easy for me to bulldoze him flat, and because it could hardly pay him to do otherwise, he morosely agreed to accept my decision.

Usually a small taxpayer finds me more sympathetic, since I'm a middle-income man myself. I've listened with great pity to hundreds of little people's complaints of inequities in the tax system. Each time, I've wished I had the power to change the law.

The oil-depletion allowance may be the most famous and most grumped-about loophole for the rich. Under the law an oil investor can deduct substantial amounts of money from his income because he is held to be depleting his reserves of oil in the ground. The law assumes that his well will run out of oil if he keeps pumping it long enough. With what I take to be astounding generosity, the law gives him a sweet tax break to compensate him in advance for that future day when the well runs dry. He can keep claiming his depletion allowance year after year, long after the total allowance has exceeded his total costs in drilling and operating the well.

Obviously, this is a deal for the very rich. The middle-income man can get in on it only indirectly and only on a minute scale, by buying a participating interest in an oil-exploration venture, or in certain other industries that get similar, though smaller, depletion allowances.

Several taxpayers have asked me—some in jest, some quite seriously—why a man can't get a depletion allowance on his own aging brain. A struggling middle-aged artist I once audited grew eloquent on the subject. "My brain and eyes and hands are to me what oil reserves are to an oil man," he protested. "They are wearing out. I'm depleting them, for God's sake. When they are gone, I'm finished. Why does the law weep for oil men but not for me? Is oil more important than art?"

But the depletion allowance, despite all the criticism it gets, is not a major inequity in the sense that large numbers of the rich can take advantage of it. In this sense, such oddities as the capital-gains tax are far more important—more damaging to the morale of less affluent citizens and, in the long run I think, to the welfare of the nation.

The most common inequity of all is one that few people ever grumble about, probably because it is so deeply embedded in our tax traditions. It has been going on since the First World War. It is the peculiar practice of subtracting certain allowable deductions from *income* instead of directly from *taxes*.

Take the common dependency exemption, for example. The law says you may deduct from your taxable income a certain sum of money for yourself and for each of your qualified dependents. This sum was $600 when I first started working for the Revenue Service. It is now up to $750 and will probably jump to $1,000 within a few years. Like many other odd little pieces of our tax law, which piously claims to give the best breaks to the poorest citizens, this one works backward. The poorer you are, the less you get out of it.

For simplicity, let's suppose the exemption is $1,000. If you are struggling along in a 20% tax bracket, each of your exemptions saves you $200 in taxes. If you are in the affluent 70% bracket, each exemption saves you $700.

Does it make sense? Not to me. It would make sense— and would be in keeping with the principle of a truly progressive income tax—if the exemption were subtracted directly from the taxes a man or woman owes. The dollar amount of the exemption could be made considerably smaller so as not to result in any net loss of revenue for the Treasury. The amount could be, let's say, $350. You would figure out your basic tax for the year (we could call this your "gross tax" or "unadjusted tax" if we wanted to continue the practice of having official labels for everything) and then you would subtract your dependency exemptions from that figure.

The result would be a better deal for the downtrodden masses—meaning me, among others. Let's suppose a middle-income man has an "unadjusted tax" of $3,000. He has four exemptions: himself, his wife and two kids. This gives him an exemption total of $1,400. He subtracts that figure from his taxes and cuts his bill by nearly a half.

To the rich man with an unadjusted tax of $50,000, the exemptions would mean less, which, I take it, is the way a progressive income tax is supposed to work. This rich taxpayer, if he had the same four exemptions, could cut his tax bill only by an insignificant percentage.

Our income-tax law started out by trying to be fair. Special-interest groups immediately began badgering Congress about inequities as felt by each group. Congress tried to soothe everybody by adding a new piece of law here and a new piece there. The law slowly became riddled with loopholes, exceptions, and exceptions to the exceptions. As the nation and its society and its financial affairs grew more complicated, so did the Internal Revenue Code. Like a tangled mass of overgrown shrubbery around an old house, the law lost its original symmetry. The fine design in the minds of the early planners became more and more obscure as the years passed, then vanished almost completely. Looking at the Code today, we gaze baffled at a dense jungle that seems not to have any clear-cut design or even any clear purpose.

Tax planners sometimes talk dreamily of tearing out all this old shrubbery and starting again from bare earth. They dream of an Internal Revenue Code so simple, so direct, so clean in its lack of loopholes and exceptions that the whole law could be written in a single thin pamphlet. This is only a dream, however. It can't be realized. Large, complicated nations must have large, complicated tax laws. I know of no historical exceptions to this frustrating rule, nor can I conceive of any way to dodge the rule in the future.

But if we can't rip out all the shrubbery and start again with a few neat little bushes, at least we can prune what we've got. We can prune enough to reveal the original design: an income tax which, insinuating itself into the economic environment where people are struggling for security, throws most of its weight behind those who haven't made it yet.

Chapter 7

THE
SECRET
RIVER

Not only can the rich escape taxes legally (avoidance, as the CPAs are pleased to call it), they can also do it illegally (evasion). Their cheating opportunities are vastly greater than those of the middle-income paycheck man, so much greater that the rich might almost be said to live under an entirely different set of laws.

I've said before that an ordinary waged or salaried man has only minor opportunities to cheat. In a typical year I can find out exactly what this man's principal income was, merely by checking the W-2 sent into IRS by his employer. Of course it can happen that our copy of his W-2 gets lost (at IRS we lose more pieces of paper per year than most organizations generate), but the man can't know it is lost at the moment when he is filling out line 11 of his Form 1040. He has no sensible choice but to state his wage or salary truthfully and attach his own copy of the W-2. He can cheat on a small scale by moonlighting for types of income that people aren't likely to report— painting people's houses, for instance, or fixing their TV sets, or selling antiques. He can play a few other little tax games, which we'll consider in a later chapter. But as far as his main income goes, I've got him by the tail.

With the rich, it's like hunting in the dark. Nobody fills out W-2s on the main incomes of the rich.

There are other types of information forms that come in, of course. There are forms telling us about fees and royalties, bank interest, stock dividends. Bits and pieces of a wealthy man's income will also show up on other taxpayers' returns. If a company collects a million dollars by transporting iron ore, that amount will show up in the form of expense deductions in other companies' tax accounts. But the task of gathering together and cross-checking all these bits and pieces of data on any given fat cat is absolutely overwhelming. Once in a while, a special agent will do it in the course of a fraud investigation, when he is convinced the work will pay off. It may take him more than a year. Most of the time we don't do it because we can't.

I'll show you in a later chapter that IRS is perhaps the world's most powerful investigative agency. No matter. Much happens that we can't see. An enormous secret river of wealth flows underneath this country, through caverns measureless to man and the Revenue Service. It won't matter what reforms are accomplished and legal loopholes closed by the President over the next few years. Even if he actually accomplishes everything he has talked about (a possibility for which I have small hope), the secret river will continue to flow unabated. Not only does nobody know how to stem it, nobody even knows how to find it.

The most notorious tributary of this river is organized crime. I don't know if it is the biggest single tributary, but it is certainly huge. Income from narcotics, prostitution, illegal gambling, loan-sharking and other Mafia enterprises is tax-free. It isn't supposed to be. "Congress can tax what it also forbids," Justice Oliver Wendell Holmes asserted. But before we can tax it, we've got to find it. It is rare that we even get a glimpse.

Only a small percentage of wealthy tax evaders are members of the Mafia, of course. But the activities of the Mafia offer an excellent illustration of tax-dodging as the game is played in the upper-income strata. A major racketeer, in his attempts to hide from my colleagues and me, behaves essentially like any rich man trying to hide. He faces the same problems. He must find answers to the same questions of what to do about undeclared income in wholesale amounts.

In this chapter I'm going to tell you about a single case involving a narcotics entrepreneur and the Internal Revenue Service. I present this case because it gives me an opportunity to generalize from the particular. The case shows how tough it is even for a huge, strong agency like IRS to find the hidden incomes of the wealthy. Whether those incomes are from narcotics or from more socially accepted types of businesses, our difficulties and frustrations are the same.

Read it and weep, dear friend and middle-income TP.

The Internal Revenue Service often gets recruited into federal "strike forces" against organized crime. One reason is that in many cases tax evasion is the only charge that can be made to stick. A racketeer may be suspected of many things, but those conducting the investigation may despair of proving anything except that the naughty fellow has made a lot of money and paid too little tax. Even this much is always difficult to prove in a courtroom and may be impossible to prove. And when we do prove it, we still end with the strong feeling—almost the certainty —that we have only seen the top of a possibly enormous iceberg. We may convict a man for hiding a million dollars of income, but we can suspect he banked another 10 or 50 million that we haven't even smelled. Also, of course, though we nail one criminal income earner, we can be perfectly sure great crowds of other nontaxpayers like him are still on the loose. How many are there, and how much tax do they evade per year? I know only that the total is colossal.

The story I want to tell began long before I got into it. An informer tipped the FBI that a certain suburban restaurant owner was a major heroin importer. He bore a nickname something like Small Joseph. According to the FBI's tipster, Small Joseph regularly bought high-quality Burmese horse (heroin) in quantity, either in France or from a French source in New York, and sold it into the distribution channels of his home city. The restaurant, said the informant, was only a front designed to give Small Joseph a visible means of support.

The FBI considered its informant reliable. Because of this, and because various federal and state agencies had been harboring suspicions of Small Joseph for other reasons, an investigation began.

For more than a year, federal and state agents watched Small Joseph's activities and quietly poked into his banking and other records, all without his knowledge. Their suspicions increased, but they found not one handful of evidence that could stand up in court.

Undercover agents sat around in bars and saw Small Joseph consorting with known underworld figures, both in New York and in his home city. This was interesting but not useful. A man is known by the company he keeps, but it is not a crime to have friends, no matter who the friends are.

Other agents followed him to Europe and back. With the cooperation of French authorities, they secretly searched his luggage at Orly Airport and his hotel room in Paris. They found nothing useful, which was about what they expected. A major importer almost never carries the merchandise personally—for a couple of thousand bucks he can hire somebody else to take that risk. If he can find an addict in bad enough need but mentally sharp, the addict will do the job for the price of a few fixes and a round-trip airplane ticket.

Small Joseph was an extremely careful man; almost paranoid in his precautions, in fact. Agents tapped his telephones and bugged his restaurant office, but they never heard any conversations even remotely relevant to narcotics. They heard certain recurrent phrases—"How's Charlie making out in Schenectady?"—and they suspected these might be part of a code. But if a code existed, they never cracked it. They saw Small Joseph spend a lot of time in telephone booths—never the same one twice—and guessed he transacted most of his business that way.

After this kind of surveillance had been going on fruitlessly for about a year, the Internal Revenue Service was called in on the game. The thought was that we might be able to close down Small Joseph's narcotics business by getting him jailed for criminal tax fraud, but this wasn't going to be an easy job. A tax-fraud case never is. To prove fraud you must not only prove that a TP underdeclared his taxable income, but you must also prove to a court's satisfaction that he did it *willfully* to evade taxes. That second requirement, dealing as it does with a man's state of mind, is so tough that we don't go after fraud convictions very often. When we catch a taxpayer short, we tend to go along with his protestations that the deficiency resulted from forgetfulness, ignorance of the law or some other benign failing. We may not believe him, but we usually don't want to get involved in a fraud case any more than he does.

There are various ways of proving fraudulent intent, most of them difficult. Courts have generally agreed that there are a number of earmarks or "badges" of fraud in tax cases, and before a U.S. Attorney will agree to carry such a case into court, the IRS agents on the case must satisfy him that one or more of these badges can be demonstrated clearly. Among the badges: deliberately destroying or falsifying records (usually tough to prove); refusing to show obviously relevant records to a revenue agent; running a business or maintaining a bank or stockbroker account under an alias; hoarding cash in large quantities without a good explanation; perpetrating the same type of falsehood on tax returns for several years in a row; and failing to declare so large a portion of income that the sheer size of the falsehood makes it look like something other than an innocent oversight.

This last badge is among those most frequently used against organized-crime figures, and as IRS began mulling over the case of Small Joseph it was generally assumed that this would probably be our main weapon against him.

The first step, however, was to prove that he did in

fact have a lot of undeclared income. Since the narcotics business is almost entirely a business of secret cash transactions, this would be a difficult proposition, too. Special agents assigned to the investigation figured the best first step would be to try for what we call a "net-wealth case" against the man. Boiled down to its essentials, a net-wealth case is one in which we demonstrate that a man's net wealth has risen faster during a certain period of years than can be explained by his reported income. We compare the then and now values of all his bank accounts, stocks, cash, real estate and other valuables (those we can find, that is) and we show that he has grown richer faster than would be possible for a man in the financial position portrayed on his tax return.

Looking over Small Joseph's tax returns, the agents found nothing seriously amiss. He declared his personal income from the restaurant business at about $30,000 in peak years and had always paid his taxes on that stated income like a good boy. The only internal inconsistency on his returns—not even an inconsistency, just an eye-catching fact—had to do with his home in the suburbs. He deducted a hefty annual real-estate tax on that home. This fact indicated that the home was expensive, perhaps somewhere in the $250,000 range. However, he deducted no mortgage interest, indicating that he owned the home free and clear. He had evidently bought it with spot cash. Where did the cash come from? Presumably a man so cautious would have a satisfactory explanation ready, but it seemed like a good idea to hear what that explanation was. Accordingly, I was assigned to audit Small Joseph's return.

It isn't common for a revenue agent to be pulled into a fraud investigation in this way. However, there was as yet no real evidence of fraud. The entire investigation to date had been little more than a fishing expedition. More-over, it seemed wise not to frighten Small Joseph at this stage. If a special agent called on him, he and his lawyer and accountant would know something serious was going on. But if the caller was only a kindly revenue agent, they might be lulled into believing this was merely a routine audit of the restaurant business.

The accountant wanted me to conduct the audit at his office, but I wanted to meet Small Joseph in person, so I said IRS preferred to have me do my work at the tax-payer's place of business. (There actually is such a rule, though it is often ignored.) And so, one Monday morning, I drove to the restaurant.

It was an expensive-looking establishment, with a lot of exposed pine beams and fieldstone and glass. Small Joseph wasn't there when I arrived. The accountant and I worked through the morning in Small Joseph's hand-somely furnished office at the rear of the building. The audit went routinely, for the accountant was good at his job and he and Small Joseph had kept meticulous records through the years. Still hoping to meet the boss, I man-aged to invent a few minor questions that the accountant couldn't answer. Small Joseph was summoned, and he turned up in the middle of the afternoon.

He was as his nickname suggested—small. That was the only thing about him that didn't surprise me. I don't know exactly what I had been expecting, a sinister and shifty-eyed criminal type, perhaps. I must have been watching too many television dramas about Treasury agents. Small Joseph was in fact a pleasant-looking man of about 35, with dark wavy hair and the kind of face that I believe is called "boyish" and "open." He was as meticu-lous in his personal grooming as in his tax accounts. He wore a white shirt and a conservative dark blue suit. He had small diamond cuff links and a matching tiepin that twinkled in the light but couldn't be called flashy. There was a certain quality of reserve about him and he wasn't talkative, yet he wasn't taciturn either. He was perfectly friendly and cooperative. He behaved as though he had nothing in the world to hide.

When I asked my question about his quarter-million-dollar house, he explained easily that he had inherited the wealth from his father, a jewelry merchant. The inheritance had been in the form of industrial stocks, he said. Since he didn't trust the stock market, he had preferred to transfer the wealth to real estate. "My feeling about real estate is that there's no sense owning it if you can't enjoy it," he explained. "So I put the whole bundle into the place that became my home."

He and the accountant promised they would show me the records pertaining to this inheritance the following day, and I had no doubt that they would be able to do so. In the light of what I had been hearing about Small Joseph, I could guess that the $250,000 was not really an inheritance but narcotics money. But I doubted I would be able to prove it. If a man has a big wad of hidden wealth and wants to bring part of it into the open (which he must do before he can enjoy it), one not too difficult approach is to rig up a fake inheritance. To do this, he must wait until a family member conveniently dies. He must then pay a few people to falsify some records. A friendly or money-hungry stockbroker is ideal for the purpose. The "heir" must also pay estate taxes. This is expensive, but the total cost of the transaction may be less than if he had declared the hidden wealth in the beginning and paid income taxes on it. At any rate, the gambit allows him to bring ill-gotten money into the open with reasonable safety.

On the following day the accountant came up with the documents to show that the alleged inheritance had taken place. I made a mental note to check on this story further, but I doubted I would find any holes in it. I now knew for certain that I was up against a supremely careful man.

Small Joseph turned up at the restaurant once more while I was finishing the audit. He had a gorgeous blonde girl with him. His tax return said he was married, but I didn't think this girl was his wife. She was about 20 years old and had startling light-green eyes. I was amused to notice that her earrings had apparently been designed to match Small Joseph's cuff links.

I finished the audit and went away feeling dissatisfied. I had turned up nothing new.

A special agent and I now began quietly looking around for hidden bank or brokerage accounts in which Small Joseph might be stashing his narcotics income. I was pessimistic, for I had developed considerable respect for Small Joseph's caution. Many rich men hide income in banks or brokerage accounts, often under aliases, and most of them get away with it most of the time. But there is always a chance of being caught, and I did not believe Small Joseph would want to take that chance. It was not in his character to leave anything to chance.

If you put secret money into an interest-bearing bank account under your own name, you can give yourself away. The bank is required to send IRS an information form telling us how much interest your money earned, and in doing so, of course, the bank reveals the existence of the money. You can't hide income safely that way. Of course you can always hope that the bank's information form will get lost, which happens often enough. You can hope, too, that IRS won't automatically cross-check the information form against your tax return, which is also a very reasonable hope; our cross-checking system isn't perfect, even with computers working round the clock. Yet you are taking a definite risk.

To avoid that risk you might try to set up an interest-earning account under an alias. You give the bank a false name, address and Social Security number. This increases your safety, but it is tricky. At the end of the year the bank sends IRS an information form bearing your pseudonym, John Doe. Since John Doe doesn't exist, he files no tax return. His name will be stored with a list of other apparent nonfilers—there are hundreds of thousands every year—and eventually (perhaps only after several years) an agent will come snooping around your bank to find out who John Doe really is. From that moment on, you won't be able to get to your money without giving yourself away.

To get around this problem some rich nontaxpayers play the bank-hopping game. To play this game you put your hidden money into a savings bank on January 1, under a false name. On December 31 you withdraw it, plus the year's interest. Sometime between then and April the bank cranks out an information return bearing your alias. By that time you are long gone, and your money is in a different bank under a different alias.

This game is successful for many, though it is not without its risks. Banks are supposed to notify IRS when large withdrawals or deposits are made, especially in cash. Not all banks comply with this rule all the time, and even when they do comply IRS doesn't always react rapidly, or at all. But the risk does exist. While you are standing at the teller's window, waiting for your withdrawal to be processed, a special agent just might be speeding down to the bank to have a chat with you.

Still another gambit is to bank untaxed money in the name of a nominee or a corporation artfully designed to mask your identity. This involves risk, too. The nominee or the corporation must file tax returns. In an audit, a key question would be: "How did you come into possession of all that money in the bank?"

To beat the bank problem entirely, a man can dump his hidden income into a stockbrokerage account. As long as he is careful to buy stocks that pay no dividends, IRS will receive no information about his portfolio in the normal course of events. Yet he is not perfectly safe. An agent may ask the brokerage for a list of its larger accounts and he may check the tax returns of those account holders to see whether they have been honest about their wealth. If some of the accounts are maintained under aliases, the agent will try to track the holders down as non-filers.

Hidden income can be put to work somewhat more safely in bearer bonds. These, as the name implies, are bonds that don't have the owner's name on them. Like cash, they are the property of any man who has them in his pocket. Unlike cash, they work for the owner by earning interest. Yet even they don't offer perfect safety from us alert and nosy folks at IRS. We are aware that bearer bonds are used to hide income, and we are always keenly interested in who the buyers are. We don't find all the buyers, but we find some.

It is also perfectly possible to put hidden income to work by channeling it into business ventures that operate out in the open. You do this by passing the money through several hands so as to obscure the original source. However, no such setup is foolproof. IRS doesn't know where all racketeering money goes, for example, but we have been able to uncover some of it flowing into legitimate businesses. As of mid-1971, agents were watching this kind of money operating in 68 hotel and motel companies, 50 liquor stores and store chains, 86 banking and stockbrokerage companies, 217 restaurant and bar operations, 71 construction companies and a host of other businesses. This was undoubtedly just a small part of the total money flow from organized crime, but the fact that we can see some of it means that the gambit is less than totally risk-free.

The really risk-free approach is to hide secret income in the form of cash: small bills that can be spent without attracting attention. Cash doesn't earn income for its owner, of course, but he may feel this is a sacrifice he must make for the sake of safety. Knowing the kind of man Small Joseph was, I felt nearly certain that this would be his solution. He would keep his money in cash. He would make no attempt to put it to work for him in the United States. He would carry it to Europe, bury it in a secret bank account and put it to work from there.

Switzerland and Liechtenstein offer the best-publicized and most useful banking services for this purpose. In those countries commercial law forbids a banker to reveal details of a client's affairs, even to a government agency under most circumstances. Even the identities of banking clients are hidden by means of the world-renowned numbered accounts.

But it isn't actually necessary to go to Switzerland or Liechtenstein if you want to hide money. In practice, you can deposit it in almost any European bank or brokerage with a fair degree of safety, or in the Near East, Latin

America or other parts of the capitalist world. The bank may make reports to its own government, but it is not likely those reports will be forwarded routinely to the U.S. Internal Revenue Service. Though we have pacts and understandings with various foreign governments, the fact is that those governments don't work very hard for us. Nor, I must say, do we for them.

Nor are IRS's own overseas operations very effective. We maintain foreign posts in key financial cities such as Bonn and London, but the posts are all understaffed, some of them critically. And even the best-staffed ones have trouble securing all the cooperation they could wish from foreign governments; no nation's bankers want foreign tax agents snooping through their records. The same goes for stockbrokers, real-estate brokers and other groups that deal with big amounts of money.

A wealthy American can hide income abroad without much difficulty, even though, unlike the narcotics business, his income-earning activity is conducted openly. There are a thousand different approaches. One common gambit is to set up a fake foreign corporation in a business related to whatever business you are conducting in America. The foreign company bills your American company for imaginary goods or services that nobody has any intention of delivering. You dutifully pay the bills, deducting that cost from your taxable U.S. income. You have thus siphoned money abroad, untaxed. You bury the money in a foreign financial institution where no IRS agent will be able to make a net-worth case out of it.

Another ploy is to rig up a phony foreign company, loan it money from America and have it default or go bankrupt. You deduct the bad debt from your taxable

U.S. income, and once again you have siphoned untaxed money abroad.

Still another approach is to find a friendly foreign banker who, for a small cut in the winnings, will agree to tell American tax authorities that he loaned you a lot of money at a stiff rate of interest. You "repay" into his bank, deducting the alleged interest from your taxable income. Again, you have slipped a lot of money past the U.S. tax man. Your only problem, as before, is to make sure that the interest you never paid doesn't show up as part of your visible wealth in the United States.

If your U.S. income is hidden to begin with—as is always the case with income from crime—you need not go through any complicated steps such as these. You simply take or send the money abroad. Once you have it safely stashed in a Swiss bank, you can repatriate it to America if that is your wish. You can, for example, decide to start a new business in America. When a revenue agent comes around and asks where you got the million dollars of capital to launch the business, you smilingly reply that it came from a wealthy Swiss investor named Hans.

Hans is in fact a Swiss stock-market operator who, temporarily down on his luck and in need of quick cash, has agreed to pose as your investor in consideration of a few thousand francs. In a private room at your bank in Zurich, you transferred slightly more than four million francs to his account, while he simultaneously gave you a certified check for that amount less his fee. You brought the check home to America and deposited it to the account of your new-born business.

IRS agents can track the check all the way through the U.S. banking system and back to Switzerland. They may even talk to good old Hans himself. But when they try to find out who Hans really is and where he got four million francs, they will find their trail dead-ended. Swiss banking authorities will shrug and say, "We sympathize with your problem, but we are afraid your questions are legally unanswerable. Hans's banking affairs are Hans's business, not ours and certainly not yours. *Auf Wiedersehen.*"

So you end with a business that you can operate openly in America. If it succeeds you live happily off its income. Your only problem is to make sure that, as far as IRS can tell, the proper proportion of the income is flowing overseas to Hans, the principal stockholder.

Since I was nearly certain that Small Joseph was holding his narcotics income in cash and that he planned to do something like this with it, I didn't hunt wholeheartedly for bank accounts, brokerage accounts or other wealth held in his name in the United States. The likelihood that we would find any such wealth seemed slim to me. Nevertheless, I went through the motions. For example, the special agent and I asked the local postmaster to give us a weekly list of everybody from whom Small Joseph received mail. If he had bank or brokerage accounts in his own name, they might show up this way.

None did show up, however. He received mail from banks, brokerages and other business connections that he had told me about openly, but from no others. This didn't necessarily mean that he wasn't doing business with others: A cautious man can maintain a secret brokerage account that no postmaster will ever discover; he simply instructs the broker not to mail account statements or other material to him. Or he can maintain an account in a city far from his home and have the statements mailed to a post-office box or the home of a friend. The trick of secretly scanning a man's mail can yield clues for an investigating agent, but it can't be trusted to tell the whole story, especially not the story of a careful man. The agent can never know what part of the iceberg he is seeing.

While we were watching our quarry's mail and poking around elsewhere behind his back, other agents followed him for several weeks. They learned nothing except that he spent a lot of time with the green-eyed girl. He was not seen to visit any financial institution except the ones he had openly declared. Nor did he do anything else to suggest the existence of hidden wealth.

Then a possible break came our way. A large number of known underworld figures, including Small Joseph, gathered at a resort hotel for what appeared to be a week's stay. A Narcotics Bureau informer reported that a major heroin buy was rumored to be in progress. Several dozen agents from various bureaus, including IRS, rushed to the scene.

The guessing among our special agents was that Small Joseph was about to sell some newly imported horse to distributors. The agents would have liked to catch him in the act, but this was impossible. Meetings among the underworld executives took place mainly in rooms on the hotel's upper floors. Women agents posed as hotel maids, and men posed as bellhops and other employees, but this gained them nothing. They never knew in advance where a meeting would be held; nor did they know where the heroin was. The hotel corridors were patrolled by petty hoodlums acting as guards, and if any suitcases or packages were moved from room to room, the agents never saw it happen. The consensus in the strike force was that it was best to wait, rather than raid the meetings at random and perhaps find nothing and blow everybody's cover. Each group of agents could then follow their own particular quarry as he left the hotel and, if they were lucky, catch him with incriminating evidence. In our case, the special agents' hope was that they could catch Small Joseph with a big bundle of money.

They guessed it would have to be big physically. Almost the entire working capital of the narcotics business is in bills of small denomination. The street pusher gets fives, tens and twenties from his clients. He uses this cash to buy the merchandise from his local distributor. The local distributor, in turn, uses the same cash to buy from a regional distributor or an importer. At no point in this chain of transactions does anybody either deposit the cash in a bank or change the small bills for large ones. There is no good reason to bring the money out into open channels of commerce where people will make records of it and ask questions about it. If an importer has a package of heroin to sell, his payment will generally be in the form of a suitcase of cash.

When Small Joseph checked out of the hotel with his girl friend, he had three suitcases and a small attaché case with him. The agents followed his cab to the airport, where they learned he and the girl had booked a flight to Paris.

The agents had to work fast. One of them got himself a seat on the plane and followed Small Joseph aboard. Small Joseph carried his attaché case with him. He had checked the three suitcases. The other agents arranged to have the takeoff delayed so they could look into the suitcases.

They found clothes.

Their attention now focused on the attaché case. It was not big enough to carry any huge amount of cash in small bills. Could the money be in large bills? Hundreds, perhaps?

The agents phoned the French customs bureau and asked that the attaché case be examined with care when Small Joseph arrived at Orly. The agent on board the plane, filled in on these facts and speculations with a note delivered by a stewardess, watched the attaché case nervously all the way across the Atlantic. Small Joseph kept it under the seat in front of him, with his feet on it. When the plane landed, the agent jostled his way to a position directly behind Small Joseph and the girl in the customs-inspection line. He noticed several men standing around the inspection table with studied nonchalance. He recognized one, an American IRS agent. The trap had been properly prepared.

The inspector asked Small Joseph to open the case. Small Joseph obeyed without hesitating.

The case contained some miscellaneous papers, letters, a small camera and a copy of the *Wall Street Journal.*

The demoralized agents skulked around behind Small Joseph for the next several days. He had a few visitors at his hotel, but beyond that he seemed to transact little business. He and the girl mostly stayed by themselves, behaving like any other pair of American tourists in Paris. They visited restaurants, a fashion salon, a couple of high-priced jewelry stores and some art galleries.

Then, suddenly, Small Joseph wasn't there. An agent had followed him and the girl to a small café. The agent didn't want to go in. He feared he would be too conspicuous. He guessed Small Joseph had begun to suspect he was being followed and had started to recognize faces recurring in crowds. The guess was probably correct. The agent waited outside the café for an hour, then saw the girl come out by herself. He went in. Small Joseph was not there. The café had a back door, leading to an alley, leading to another street.

Small Joseph rejoined the girl two days later, looking relaxed and happy. Where had he been? To bury his wealth in a secret bank account?

This was what the agents suspected, but there was one question they were never able to answer. *How had he brought the wealth to Europe?*

It was conceivable that at those meetings in the resort hotel back in America he had been paid for the heroin with a check drawn on a European bank—a check that we at IRS could never trace. Conceivable, but not likely. Such a transaction would be a departure from the normal pattern of the U.S. narcotics trade. The distributors who were buying the merchandise from him would wish to pay in cash. Cash was their safest form of working capital. It was the only form that left no tracks. It was the form they were used to, the form in which they themselves were paid. Before they could pay Small Joseph with a check, they would have to take the extra risk of depositing their capital in a bank. They might bury their profits that way, but not their operating money. Even the Swiss and Liechtensteiners will open a secret bank account if convinced it contains clues to a major crime. Would the distributors accept that extra degree of risk?

No, the most likely guess was that Small Joseph had been paid in cash. If so, was it conceivable he had hired somebody else to carry the cash to Europe for him?

Again, conceivable but not likely. He could hire somebody else to carry his heroin, for heroin in large quantities isn't easily negotiable. He could be reasonably sure the carrier wouldn't try to run off with the merchandise, especially if guarded. But cash is different. If somebody hands you a suitcase containing half a million dollars in small bills, you might be strongly tempted to vanish. If guards have been posted to watch you, you are in a position to tempt them just as strongly. Cash is the ultimate in negotiable wealth. Would a supremely careful man like Small Joseph trust luck and human nature to that extent? It didn't seem plausible.

Yet, if this reasoning was sound, where had the money gone? Small Joseph had not left it at the resort hotel in America. The hotel rooms and office safe were searched after the meetings, and neither heroin nor cash turned up. Many of the known racketeers were searched—illegally, they said—but without success. Only two packages of heroin were found, both being carried from the hotel by young men previously unknown to either the local police or the federal agents. Both were quickly bailed out of jail by wealthy "friends." There was nothing with which to catch the big fish—and that included IRS's own particular big fish, Small Joseph.

Meanwhile I had been taken off the case and returned to my normal duties. But I kept thinking about Small Joseph, wondering about him, picking up snatches of news about him. And one day months later, while I was having a glass of beer with one of the special agents, a startling thought came to me. The special agent was mumbling about Small Joseph's green-eyed girl friend, who seemed to have made a considerable impression on every agent involved in the case, including me. She was indeed a stunning girl. The agent remarked that he could understand why Small Joseph spent so much money on her.

I said, "Jewelry."

He said, "What?"

"Gems," I said. "In Paris, didn't he take her to a couple of jewelry places?"

"Sure, among others. Bought her a fur wrap, too."

I recalled being impressed by Small Joseph's diamond cuff links and tiepin and the girl's earrings. I also recalled his offhand remark that his father had been in the gem business. Might it be that Small Joseph knew a lot about precious stones—how to assess them, where to sell them?

"Just for fun," I said, "find out if there were any known jewel fences at that resort hotel. Anybody with a record of handling stolen gems. Or anybody at all in the gem business."

The special agent saw the point and went off to make some phone calls. We got our answer a day later. The answer was yes. At least one of the racketeers attending the meetings was on record as a receiver of stolen jewelry. Another man in the hotel at the same time—perhaps an innocent citizen, perhaps not—was a wealthy Dutch diamond merchant.

Now we thought we saw the picture. If you want to carry a lot of wealth inconspicuously in a small space—your pockets, your girl's handbag—one feasible approach would be to convert the wealth into jewelry or unset gems.

There was no way to tell exactly how Small Joseph had worked the gambit. The one thing we were almost sure of was that this artful taxpayer, *even while being watched*, had managed to make off with a magnificent pile of untaxed wealth and hide it.

His wealth has joined the secret river. I presume he is still being watched by one bureau or another, but I am not optimistic about the outcome. Not even IRS, one of the most powerful investigative agencies in the history of the world, has much hope of closing in on this clever and careful man.

Clever, careful and rich. A man like that, if he doesn't like income taxes, can almost always find a way to escape them.

Chapter 8

BRIBERY AND THE REVENUE AGENT

The U.S. Internal Revenue Service, which is very good at getting information out of people, is also very good at keeping information from them. It is a marvel of clever public relations, I think, that IRS has generally kept the public from talking about a subject that comes up again and again in private conversations among revenue folk. The subject is bribery.

Consider. A revenue officer (collection division), revenue agent (audit), or special agent (intelligence) commonly comes into his job at the Civil Service level of GS-5 or GS-7, depending on his college performance and other qualifications. The pay for a GS-5 is $7,319 a year; for a GS-7, $9,053. If the man does his job well and pleases his superiors, he can be promoted to GS-9 in one year and win a salary raise to slightly over $11,000. After two years, if he is lucky, he can go up to GS-11 and earn a little more than $13,000. The very most he can hope for in his wildest dreams is eventual promotion to an executive level and a salary somewhere above $30,000. But the vast majority of agents quit the service for more lucrative jobs before even reaching the level of $20,000.

Not only is the pay low, but the opportunities for outside earnings are minimal. All IRS employees are strongly discouraged from moonlighting. They are positively forbidden to take any outside employment that would cause a conflict of interest with their revenue jobs—to work in accounting offices, for example, or to free-lance as tax-return preparers. They are required to ask permission before taking any other kind of job, and the permission is usually denied. Of course many revenue people do hold outside jobs secretly, but this makes life very difficult for them, much more so than for moonlighting policemen or teachers. Every revenue employee's tax returns are subject to careful and regular scrutiny, and the only secret employment he can get is the type in which his employer sends no information to IRS. He can mow people's lawns, and that's about the limit of his opportunities.

Now picture a revenue agent, salaried at $13,000, auditing the returns of a wealthy taxpayer to whom $13,000 is mere pocket money. Suppose the audit shows a tax deficiency of $50,000. Speaking from a strictly economic point of view rather than a moralistic one, the taxpayer will find it about four times as pleasant to pay a $13,000 bribe rather than the $50,000 deficiency. The sum of 13 grand represents an entire year's income for the agent. What's more, it is tax-free, since neither he nor the taxpayer will make any public announcement of the transaction. Can the agent resist?

The U.S. income-tax system is probably the world's best-designed playing field for the game of bribery. It is certainly the biggest such field. It is a system in which thousands of low-salaried men and women deal directly with amounts of money so enormous as to make their eyes pop and their brains reel.

Every Internal Revenue Commissioner in history has on occasion uttered kind remarks about the high moral caliber of his organization's employees. "It is remarkable," the standard eulogy goes, "how few of these men and women succumb to temptation. . . ."

Well, yes. The record for 1971, a fairly typical year, shows that the service's internal-security gumshoes handled 499 "conduct investigations" and 2,155 "special inquiries" of IRS personnel during the year. As a result, eight people were fired directly for taking part in bribery, extortion or collusion; and 91 were fired for falsifying reports and records without provably accepting bribes. In total, 181 men and women were fired during the year for these and other types of misconduct; another 37 were suspended temporarily; and another 323 received official reprimands, warnings or demotions. These numbers aren't large in an organization with nearly 70,000 employees.

Nor are the statistics on attempted bribery large. Indeed, they are microscopic. In fiscal 1971, 134 revenue employees reported bribe offers from taxpayers, and these reports resulted in 47 arrests. Commissioner Johnnie M. Walters noted with great pride that this number, 47, was an all-time high. But when you compare it with the number of tax returns that were filed during the year—more than 110 million—it fades to insignificance. It becomes ridiculous, in fact. Of all the nation's taxpayers, fewer than one in 2.5 million was caught handing out hush money.

Are Americans really that honest? One can be excused for doubting it.

The fact is that the commissioner simply doesn't know —nor does anybody else—how many taxpayers offered bribes during the year. Nor how many agents declined without saying anything. Nor how many agents accepted. There is just no way to measure the amount of bribery and attempted bribery and extortion (in which the agent makes the suggestion to the TP) that goes on. My own guess is that the amount, if it could ever be counted and totaled in terms of dollars, would shock the nation grievously.

It is probably safe to say that every IRS field agent has had at least some experience with offered bribes. But even when an agent declines a bribe—even when the idea fills him with pious horror—he isn't likely to make a fuss about it. Typically, he will simply say no thanks and go on about his business, and nothing new will be added to the commissioner's meager store of knowledge on the subject. There are practical reasons for the agent's silence, and I can illustrate these reasons best by recalling the first bribe offer that came my way.

I was going over the books of a medium-small electrical-contracting firm. The books were a mess, and after a while I began to suspect that the mess was deliberate. Somewhere in the background I began to smell hidden income. The more I dug into the figures and the more I questioned the company's lawyer and accountant, the more certain I became that the company had taken in at least $100,000 more income during the tax year than it had reported.

The lawyer and accountant were obviously aware of the track I was on. They fidgeted. They sweated. They smoked appalling numbers of cigarettes. After a while they excused themselves and left the room. When they came back a few minutes later, the lawyer smiled at me cheerfully.

"Listen," he said, "the deeper we get into this, the more complicated it gets, right? So why should we aggravate ourselves? You're busy. I'm busy. Let's speed it up, what do you say?"

"How do you mean?" I asked, though I thought I knew the answer.

"Well, listen, what are we talking? Ten thou of tax deficiency, maybe? Twenty thou? Maybe nothing, right? You don't know, I don't know. We could go all through this and maybe you'll come out with nothing but a headache. And me, my ulcer hurts. This kind of aggravation isn't healthy for me. I'll pay a lot for good health. I mean, if this puts me in a hospital it could cost me five thou in doctor bills and lost income. I'd rather pay the five thou and stay out of the hospital. Makes sense?"

I didn't know how to react. I finally mumbled that we were all tired and ought to stop work until the next day. I went away feeling badly confused. I was young and somewhat idealistic, and the lawyer's offer shocked me. At the same time, I couldn't help translating $5,000 into hypnotically attractive things that I wanted to buy. A new car. Oh, how I needed a new car. A house. I was newly married, and a baby was on the way, and a $5,000 down payment could move my wife and me out of the crack-plastered little apartment we euphemistically called home. Five thousand dollars, tax-free . . .

But then I grew frightened. My work, like all field agents' work, was subject to review back at the office. I was fairly sure I could write an internally consistent RAR (revenue agent report) that would cover up the electrical contractor's tax deficiency, but only fairly sure, not certain. (Today, with a lot more experience behind me, I'm certain I could have done it.) I finally went into my group chief's office. "I want to report an attempted bribe," I said, melodramatically.

The group chief was a large old man with a red face and untidy white hair. He leaned back in his chair, stoked up his pipe and invited me to tell him all about it.

When I had finished he nodded. "So what do you want to do about it?" he asked.

The question seemed odd to me. "Why, prosecute, of course," I said. "Write a formal complaint, or whatever I'm supposed to do. There must be a procedure for it, isn't there?"

The chief grinned at me. "Sure, there's a procedure. But let me ask you something. How are you going to prove this bribe offer was made? You got any witnesses?"

"Well, no."

"Of course not. So it'll be your word against the TP's. A lot of nastiness, a lot of hard feeling, and nothing can come of it. Except maybe the TP will turn around and accuse you of extortion. He'll say you tried to squeeze money out of him. He refused, so you hollered bribe to cover yourself or to get revenge."

I recalled some FBI movies I'd seen. "Well," I said, "why can't I take the bribe while some special agent watches from behind a tree, or something?"

The chief took his pipe from his mouth and laughed. Then he became serious. "Look, son, you're a good agent but you've still got things to learn about this business. This office has got to keep up its production, you understand? That's what we're here for. Production. If I'm going to let my agents get tied up in court every time some TP makes noises about hush money, I'll never get any work done. I'll lose my job, you'll lose yours, and the government will lose all the tax money we're supposed to bring in. Prosecuting a bribe case won't help me and it won't help you."

"You're telling me to forget it?"

He shrugged. "I'm advising you. It's not an order. If you feel strongly enough about it—well, okay. But bear in mind that you were hired to bring in tax money. That's your main responsibility."

He was telling me, without actually saying so, that I could not win any points with him nor win any promotions or pay raises by being a hero in a bribe case. Only one thing counted as far as he was concerned. Production.

So the next day I went out and produced. I told the lawyer I was sorry about his ulcer but I really couldn't see that it was any concern of mine. And I went ahead with the audit and ended by recommending a tax deficiency of something like $30,000.

That made my group chief very happy. I was raised from GS-7 to 9 not long afterward.

The experience taught me a lesson that most revenue agents and special agents learn quite early in their careers: Heroism buys no bread and butter. In a large organization like IRS, in fact, heroism only annoys people.

Officially, of course, IRS is against bribery and in favor of motherhood, patriotism and apple pie. An agent who squeals on a bribe-minded TP gets a sentimental little letter of commendation from the commissioner. Such a letter makes a nice keepsake, though its financial value is zero. The agent can hang it on his wall to comfort him in his poverty-stricken old age. He can glory in the fulsome praise with which IRS and Justice Department officials will have showered him. The praise soars to great heights of poetry at times. U.S. Attorney Frederick B. Lacy, emerging from a successful bribery prosecution in 1971, erupted thus: "The courage and integrity of the men of the Internal Revenue Service led to this arrest. I am proud to be associated with agents who, by their shining example, have demonstrated to the cynical segment of the public that probity cannot be eroded by bribery."

His probity uneroded and his example shining brightly, the agent who squealed can perhaps find contentment. But he must know that many or most of his colleagues consider him a damned fool. Even Commissioner Walters has publicly recognized that it is not easy, and perhaps not always smart, to be a hero. "An agent who develops a bribery case despite great trial and inconvenience, rather than simply turning away from it, is serving us all," he once said, rather plaintively. He knows about the "trial and inconvenience," and he is well aware that most agents react to a bribe offer by "turning away." That is the most practical reaction. That, or acceptance of the bribe. The least practical reaction is to make a fuss.

On the pragmatic level, out in the field where the gritty work of tax collection actually takes place, an act of overt heroism or fuss-making only irritates people. The commissioner, far away in Washington, may be pleased enough to send the hero a letter of commendation. But the hero's immediate superiors, concerned with production and unwilling to fill out any more forms than are absolutely necessary, will wish the hero had kept his mouth shut.

In IRS as in any big organization, the most workable basic policy for the average employee is silence. As long as you keep quiet about what you do or don't do, only one person gets annoyed with you—yourself. It might be argued that the initial act of turning down a bribe is an act of quiet heroism, perhaps even more heroic in its way than would be the secondary act of squealing on the bribe offerer. I've known many an agent who having said no to a large wad of tax-free cash spent the next several weeks scorning himself for a fool.

One friend of mine—Harry, I'll call him—quietly got drunk in a bar one day while telling me of his troubles over a bribe. I had dropped into the bar at about 4:30 in the afternoon to have a bottle of beer before going home. I had just finished an audit in which the taxpayer had agreed to a sizable deficiency, and I felt the U.S. government could afford to give me an extra hour off. I saw Harry sitting at the bar drinking straight whiskey. Judging by the fullness of the ashtray by his elbow, he had been brooding there a long time.

"Siddown, you low-paid sucker," he said, and I knew instinctively what he was brooding about.

Poor old Harry hadn't been offered a cash bribe. Instead he had been offered a job—a $50,000-a-year sinecure. The offerer of this bribe was a multimillionaire who was the main stockholder and autocratic boss of a family-owned manufacturing business. Harry had stumbled on evidence that the man was regularly siphoning income to Europe and hiding it there, probably in Switzerland or Liechtenstein. The evidence was slight and could be easily suppressed when Harry wrote his RAR, but the millionaire obviously feared an investigation and he was willing to pay Harry generously if Harry would look the other way.

There are several effective ways to get money into a secret European bank account where it can hide from U.S. revenue agents. We looked at some in the preceding chapter. Another way is to set up a fake purchasing deal with a cooperative European businessman.

Let's say you're running an American company that manufactures widgets. The most expensive component of a widget is a gidget, and because of high labor rates in America you can buy gidgets more cheaply in Europe. You approach a German gidget maker and tell him, "I need a million gidgets a year. You want the business?"

He says, "*Jawohl.*"

You say, "Okay, if you'll do things my way, the contract is yours. Your price for gidgets is fifty dollars apiece delivered in New York, right? So I'll pay you a hundred apiece. You bank the money. When I come to Europe, you give me the extra fifty dollars back."

On your U.S. tax return at the end of the year you state that it cost you $100 million to buy a million gidgets. This amount is deductible from income. You then go to Europe where the sum of $50 million is waiting for you, untaxed, and you blow a few thousand on champagne and girls and expensive hotel suites and you hide the remainder in a numbered bank account in Switzerland or, better yet, the still more secretive Liechtenstein.

The chance that a U.S. revenue agent will uncover such a scheme, provided it is carefully and cleverly arranged, is not great. One tip-off for the U.S. agent might be that you have paid an unaccountably high price for your gidgets. By sheer bad luck he might happen to know or discover that European-made gidgets aren't supposed to cost $100 apiece. Something like this had aroused the suspicions of my friend Harry as he went over the millionaire's books.

"What would you do?" he asked me as I settled down with my beer.

"I don't know," I replied, evasively but honestly. "A

man never knows until it actually happens to him." I went on to say that I had turned down several direct bribe offers during my career, and in a number of other cases I had switched off conversations that seemed to be meandering around the subject of bribery in an exploratory way. "But who knows what I'll do next time?" I asked. "Every time I say no, I want to kick myself for being a damned fool. Next time, maybe, I'll figure I've been a fool long enough."

"One of my kids has a leaky heart valve," Harry said morosely. "The doctor and hospital bills are piling up several miles high. I ask myself who needs money more, me or the government?"

Having no useful answer to offer, I buried my face in my beer.

"And another question I ask myself," Harry said, "is which is worth more to me, my morals or my kid's heart?"

This question, too, was unanswerable. All I could do was mumble a platitude about decision-making. I advised Harry to make his decision quickly and stop tormenting himself over it.

"Whatever I decide will be wrong," Harry said, and he signaled the bartender for another drink.

A couple of weeks later I noticed that Harry wasn't around the office anymore. I asked somebody what had become of him and was told he had left the service for a job in private industry. I was glad he had made his decision. But I wished he had trusted me enough to say goodbye.

Our group chief had a few words to say on the subject a few days afterward. "It's funny the way guys leave the service," he remarked. "Often as not, the new job a guy goes to is with a company he's been auditing." The chief said this without rancor, but it was obvious he knew exactly what was going on.

The subject of bribery, much discussed within IRS,

doesn't often leak out into the public media. Once in a while some crusading congressman or reform-minded citizen such as Ralph Nader pokes and prods at the subject, but since the facts are so elusive it is rare that such an investigation produces much in the way of solid evidence. The biggest investigation in my memory took place fully 20 years ago, and hardly anything new has been said publicly in all the years since.

That scandal of the early 1950s was stirred up by John Williams, then the junior U.S. Senator from Delaware. He had been in office about a year when he learned to his surprise that he was listed with IRS as a delinquent taxpayer. It turned out that one of his tax payments had somehow vanished, though he could show canceled checks to prove he had actually made the payment. Digging into the mystery, he discovered that the payment had been embezzled by an assistant cashier at his local IRS office. The cashier's superiors had known about the embezzlement but had done nothing about it because, they later explained, they didn't want IRS's reputation besmirched in public. The cashier, in fact, had been promoted.

This incident made Williams angry. It also made him suspect that the Revenue Service was not staffed entirely by honest men. He began to dig. Taxpayers all over the country, learning of his investigation, wrote to tell him of their own unhappy experiences. Soon Williams had a pile of evidence that shocked even the complacent America of the 1950s. The Revenue Service, it turned out, was riddled with corruption; was rotten to the very core. Not only were lowly revenue agents taking bribes regularly, but so were some of the top officials.

As a result of Williams's probing, several regional chiefs of IRS (then called BIR, the Bureau of Internal

Revenue) landed in prison. One BIR executive was found to have earned some $190,000 of unexplained income during his time in office. Another man couldn't explain $160,-000. The chief counsel of BIR admitted accepting "gifts" from big taxpayers who had cases pending. A Mafia man testified that he had handed out more than $100,000 to various BIR people for tax-fixing services. And so it went.

It was like lifting an expensive rug, seeing a termite-infested floor beneath and quickly dropping the rug back in place. The Williams scandal petered out by the mid-1950s. The bureau fired some people and somehow managed to convince the public that only honest employees would be hired from then on. This unlikely promise seemed to satisfy nearly everybody, for Americans in those smug and boomish years preferred not to dwell on thoughts that might upset their tranquility. "Who cares?" went the popular philosophy. "Where there's money, there's corruption. It's human nature. There's nothing we can do about it, so let's all relax." The nation did relax, and IRS since then has managed to prevent a scandal of that size and scope from erupting again. The rug has stayed down, and only those who work around IRS know what the floor beneath is really like.

I can remember being shocked more than once in the starry-eyed beginnings of my career. At one small field office where I was assigned briefly, the group chief and assistant chief used to hand out cases on the basis of seniority. Young agents like me got the simplest cases, or were assigned in teams to audit the tax returns of big companies. Big companies seldom offer bribes, and publicly owned ones almost never do, for no executive wants to take the responsibility. And why should he? It isn't his money; it's the stockholders'. The most likely sources of bribes are wealthy individuals and small, privately owned or closely held companies. The group chief and assistant chief always saved such cases for themselves.

"Hey-hey, look at the T&E on this one!" the chief would say to the assistant chief. "You want it?"

"I'll take it!" the assistant chief would say, grabbing hungrily. T&E, or travel and entertainment, is an area of nearly universal cheating and a rich source of potential hush money to any predatory agent.

When I first heard my superiors talking this way I couldn't believe what my innocent young ears were hearing. I thought charitable thoughts. "Well," I told myself, "maybe they love their work so much that they want the most complicated cases for themselves." Later I grew more cynical. I deduced that like almost everybody else in this hungry world what they really loved was money.

I hope for, yet fear, the day when another Williams-style crusader lifts the rug again. The likelihood is that if such a scandal did break out now it would have more important consequences for IRS than did Williams's efforts. This is a more sharply critical, self-questioning era. Under a strong enough attack IRS might have to be rebuilt from the ground up. Either that, or this whole mad system of taxation by self-assessment might have to be abandoned in favor of a better and fairer revenue-raising idea.

We have already seen that the rich escape taxes through loopholes, through their ability to take advantage of deals such as low capital-gains taxes and tax-free bonds and through being able to hire the smartest lawyers and accountants. They also escape taxes, on occasion, by being able to offer the juiciest bribes in the subtlest ways.

What can a middle-income man offer me that will

tempt me? Hardly anything I can think of. I remember one man in the $15,000-a-year bracket whose tax return said he had six children. I audited him at his home, and the first thing that puzzled me was that the home was a little one-story ranch. I wondered where he would fit six kids. The next thing I noticed was that there was no kid clutter lying around: no bikes, no toys, no children's books. You can't easily jam six kids into a small home without having juvenile paraphernalia all over the place. I asked the taxpayer about his kids and got evasive replies, and then I made other inquiries and found that the man and his wife were in fact childless. He had invented one new kid per year for six years and might have gone on inventing them for years more if he hadn't been caught. Now the back taxes, interest and fraud penalties were going to total more than he could raise without selling his house. He was desperate, more desperate than the rich ever get, for we were talking about almost his entire net worth. He was desperate enough to offer me a bribe, very bluntly. But the paradox was that he couldn't offer what a rich man might have offered, though his need to get off the hook was far greater. Even if I had been the bribe-taking type, he could not have tempted me. The risk he was asking me to take was too great to accept for any amount of money he could command.

"Listen," he kept saying, "there must be a way out of this. What do you want? If I've got it, it's yours." He was nearly in tears.

"Stop talking nonsense," I said. "By trying to bribe me you're making things worse. Bribery is a serious offense."

"I can't get in any worse trouble than I'm already in," he said, and now there actually were tears running down his cheeks. "I'm going to lose everything I've got, everything I've built up over the years. Listen, let me pay you in installments. Suppose I were to offer you a thousand a year for ten years?"

"Cut it out, man!" I shouted at him. I recalled sadly that a Mafia lawyer had once offered me $50,000 in spot cash to cover up a tax deficiency which to him and his colleagues was far less serious in its consequences than what this middle-income taxpayer was facing. The Mafia group's tax troubles merely meant they were going to be somewhat less rich than they had been before. Yet they could offer a bribe that was worth thinking about. How could the little TP compete? I said, "Calm down. It isn't the end of the world. You may be able to make a deal with a revenue officer if you can't come up with the money all at once. Maybe he'll let you pay it in installments. He might even fifty-three it—write off some or all as uncollectable." I grinned at the man. "Cheer up. The Revenue Service doesn't want you to go bankrupt, you know. We want you to stay afloat so we can go on collecting taxes from you."

He sat slumped in his chair and nodded resignedly. "You won't make any trouble about this bribe business? I wasn't thinking straight. . . ."

"I didn't hear anything about a bribe," I said. It was the least I could do for him.

It isn't often that a bribe is offered to an agent as bluntly as that taxpayer did it. Usually there is a lot more circling around. The TP's lawyers generally start by checking out the agent, asking friends in IRS if he can be "talked to." If the answer is yes, they may test him conversationally for days or weeks before talking turkey. Even then, the agent sometimes goes away wondering if he has actually been offered a bribe at all.

If you are in tax trouble and want to try the bribe route as a means of exit, I would advise you to use the subtle rather than blunt approach. I certainly don't counsel the use of bribery as a tax loophole, but if you must use it, I urge you to use it with care. It is a dangerous technique that can backfire with extremely painful results. You may come up against a pious and fussy breed of agent who, despite the problems it will create for himself and a lot of other people, will try to make a case out of attempted bribery. The trick is to offer the bribe without offering it. The offer becomes something like a dim star in a misty night sky: You see it out of the corner of your eye, but when you stare straight at it, it isn't there.

I once conducted a week-long audit of a TV executive's tangled affairs. During the week I got into the habit of eating my lunch at a small and rather expensive restaurant around the corner from his office, and when each day's work was finished I would stop in to have a beer at the restaurant's bar before going home. On the fourth evening a stunning dark-haired girl sat at the bar next to me and ordered a vodka martini.

She opened the conversation by remarking that she liked beer in the middle of the day but not at night. Then she started to talk about the TV business. She said she was an actress. She mentioned the TV executive I was auditing and pretended to be surprised when I said I knew him. She said she liked him very much; he was a fine fellow, had a heart of gold, was ridiculously generous to his friends. Having made that point she asked me what kind of entertainment I liked. Her favorite kind, she said, was sex. She said she was tired of all the men she knew and would like to find an attractive stranger and spend a few weeks with him. She let fall the casual remark that she had a luxurious apartment not far from where we sat. Then she looked at her watch, discovered she was late for a date and stood up.

"I come in here most nights around this time," she said. "Will you be here tomorrow night?"

I said I probably would. She left.

I knew very well, and she knew I knew, what was going on. The following day I was scheduled to finish my audit of the TV man. An unpleasantly large tax deficiency was looming up. If I failed to recommend the deficiency the girl would meet me at the bar.

There is no point in telling the end of the story. If she met me, obviously I wouldn't say so.

Bribery by call girl is common because it is not risky for the taxpayer. A money bribe can be traced, while a call girl's services do not leave the kinds of tracks that can easily be followed by IRS inspectors. Moreover, such a bribe can be offered without seeming to be a bribe. The dark-haired girl said nothing that could have been hung on the TV man, and if I had tried to make a case of it I would have been laughed out of court.

Money bribes can also be offered subtly, however. One friend of mine in the service told me of a time when he audited a small department-store chain. During the audit, as he was sitting in the chain's main office with the president and a couple of accountants, a secretary walked in and handed the president a large, bulging manila envelope secured with rubber bands. The president said off-handedly that the envelope contained part of the week's cash receipts, $20,000 or so, mainly in small bills. He casually put the envelope down on the desk where the agent was working.

The audit proceeded with the fat envelope sitting there amid an untidy clutter of other envelopes, file folders and papers. It was a troublesome audit, with evidence of tax fraud in the background. At the end of the day, with the work no more than half finished, the agent got ready to go home. He began the long process of packing his briefcase. Great loads of paper go into every revenue agent's briefcase; this is among the major irritations of the job. As he was stuffing in the last few documents and forms, the company president picked up the envelope.

"This is yours, isn't it?" he asked. "Don't forget it."

The agent said no, he didn't believe it was his.

"Are you sure?" the president asked. "There's so much paper around here that I don't know which is whose."

The agent said he was sure the envelope wasn't his. The president shrugged and said, "Then I guess it's mine."

And so the matter ended. A bribe had been offered, yet not offered.

It is interesting to speculate on how many Revenue Service people succumb to this enormous temptation and how often. One cynical friend of mine believes the average agent tends to say no almost automatically, knee-jerk fashion, the first time the question comes up. But then, as time goes by, he gets mad at himself. His work takes him into rich people's homes, offices, bank records and brokerage accounts. He compares the life-styles of the wealthy with his own grubby circumstances and he vows he will say yes the next time a good, risk-free opportunity comes up.

My own observations lead me to conclude that the average agent—not every agent, just the average one—

stays honest until honesty becomes painful. As long as his financial life remains relatively calm, he's all right. But if a money emergency comes along, then a bribe offer equaling his year's salary may take him. In nearly every case where I've known or suspected that a man took hush money, there was a financial emergency in the background.

My friend Harry, the fellow who accepted the $50,000-a-year job, came around to buy me an expensive lunch not long ago. I was curious to know whether his decision had given him as much trouble after he made it as before. Was he happy?

Evidently so. "Let me tell you something," he said in a philosophical moment. "Moral pride is nice. But being able to pay your bills is nicer."

Chapter 9

THE REVENUE SERVICE: AN AMERICAN GESTAPO?

Of all the information-gathering agencies in all the world's governments, past or present, the very cleverest must surely be the United States Internal Revenue Service. This monster organization gathers more information about more people, does it more quietly and raises less public outcry in the process than any other government outfit I know anything about.

It may be that Soviet Russia or Red China can boast of agencies that beat IRS on all these counts. I strongly doubt it, but all right; since those nations' governments operate with a high degree of secrecy, I will have to grant that one or more of their agencies could contend for this crown. No other agency, however, could even come close.

The FBI, you say? Not a chance. I don't know how many citizens the FBI watches regularly, how many dossiers it keeps in its files. A few million, perhaps. At IRS, which in terms of personnel alone is about six times larger than the FBI, we keep track of nearly every income-earning teen-ager and adult in the country. We know almost everything of substance that there is to know about you, and what we don't know we can find out.

The Gestapo? Not a contender either. I doubt the Gestapo came anywhere near matching us in sheer size even when it was fully extended throughout Europe. Even if it did, the Gestapo lost the game by being too overtly aggressive and making too many enemies. It went about its work too noisily, too clumsily. The Revenue Service makes enemies, of course, but most of them cool off in a few weeks or months. There is no great or persistent public outcry against us or our methods of operation. Most citizens assume we are doing a job that needs to be done, and if we are a damned nuisance we are generally conceded to be a necessary one. Not since 1913, when Congress amended the Constitution so as to allow for an income tax, has there been any serious public discussion of the legality of such a tax or of the government's right to invade citizens' privacy in the course of collecting the tax.

We became somewhat concerned about our image in the late 1960s when radicals of the New Left were loudly grousing about the FBI and the CIA and local police departments and other data-gathering organizations. We were a little afraid that our turn would come eventually. It never did. No basic political questions about IRS have ever been raised seriously in public, except by isolated groups paddling their tiny rafts of advocacy on a vast sea of indifference. Some of our local offices have been picketed on occasion by disgruntled taxpayers griping about alleged inequities in the tax law or about the use of tax money to support the Vietnam War. But there has never been a mass demonstration against us or a concerted attempt to disrupt our operations.

This seems strange, for an agent of the Internal Revenue Service is a combination of policeman and spy, and an outrageously powerful one at that. He may be, in fact, the most powerful in the country. There is no important piece of information concerning you that I am effectively forbidden to seek.

I once audited the tax return of a very prickly college professor, a far-gone civil-libertarian, who made the mistake of throwing me a challenge. He was a man who made a political fetish out of the trappings of poverty. He habitually wore old clothes, an uncombed beard and a moth-eaten Indian headband, and in this getup he taught his sociology classes and attended protest meetings, grumbling about virtually everything. He had been to jail for several overnight stays, for it was his pleasure to bait the local police and then complain about their high-handedness in arresting him. He felt that the "establishment," as he called it, was a soft opponent. The establishment had never been able to do more than slap him lightly on the wrist. In this state of complacency, he had the misfortune to run up against the Internal Revenue Service.

There were several inconsistencies in his tax return that puzzled me. He had deducted the cost of several long automobile trips to visit real-estate properties that he owned. The existence of these properties didn't quite square with his low stated income. When I questioned him about this he answered vaguely that he had inherited the properties. Another puzzle was that two of the properties appeared to have vanished since his previous year's tax return. On that earlier return he had deducted real-estate taxes on those properties, but the same deductions did not show up on the current year's return. To a revenue agent a year-to-year change like this is a tip-off that the tax-payer may have sold property and failed to declare a capital gain. When I asked the professor what was going on, he mumbled that he had forgotten to pay the real-estate taxes on some of his properties during the latest year.

I was far from satisfied. I asked to see his bankbooks and other records. That was when he mounted his soapbox and gave me a lecture about the rights of private citizens. "I will not submit to Gestapo tactics!" he declared with high solemnity.

"You refuse to show me your records?"

"I certainly do. You have no right to pry into a citizen's private affairs like this."

It is true that an IRS agent is not supposed to conduct a fishing expedition, poking around in a taxpayer's records in the mere hope of finding something amiss. (There is really nothing to stop him from doing this if he wants to, but technically he isn't supposed to.) Where there is reason to suspect error or wrongdoing, however, the agent has very few official restrictions in his way.

I didn't argue with the professor. I simply went to his bank.

It was a small suburban bank. The president, a short plump man with a worried look, seemed distinctly unhappy to see me. As I had suspected might happen, the professor had phoned him before I got there and had instructed him not to show me anything. The professor had evidently threatened the banker with lawsuits and other calamities if the bank opened its records to me. But there are no effective banking-secrecy laws in the United States. Most banks protect the privacy of their clients' records; but this a matter of professional ethics, not law. Four times out of five, when I walk into a bank and flash my credentials I get to see anything I want to see. Some bankers are so cooperative that they border on the servile.

When they don't want to cooperate, it is seldom difficult to change their minds.

"You won't show me the records?" I asked the plump little banker.

He had pale-blue eyes and he had a habit of blinking them rapidly. He looked almost as though he were about to burst into tears. "I'd really rather not," he said. "I'd like to check with some other people around here first. I don't know what our position would be on something like this. . . ."

I nodded, then made a production of pulling a small black notebook and pen out of my inside breast pocket. "May I have your full name, sir?"

That got him. It almost always does. There is hardly an American citizen above the poverty level whose tax conscience is so completely clear that he isn't scared of being audited. I didn't actually threaten him with an audit, of course, and even the implied threat was sheer bluff; a field agent, as I said earlier, has no authority to select taxpayers for audit. But almost any IRS employee can perpetrate this kind of bluff successfully. The TP thinks, "Well, maybe it *is* a bluff, but why take chances?" Why indeed? Especially if the taxpayer has nothing to lose personally by doing what the agent wants. The little blinky-eyed banker had nothing to lose except perhaps a degree of professional pride. Faced with the choice of shooting down his client or getting shot at himself, he naturally decided the question in his own favor.

He mumbled, "Well, um, maybe we can—um." He

scurried out of the room. A few moments later he was back, brimming over with cooperation. "My secretary will show you any records you want to see," he said. "But just to protect myself—in case my customer gets mad, you know—may I ask you to serve me with an official summons first?"

It was a common request, quickly arranged.

The professor's account records revealed what I had been expecting: several large deposits that may have included undeclared capital gains, plus some regular, monthly, smaller deposits that may have been rent receipts. The records certainly showed a good deal more activity than was accounted for in the man's tax returns.

I turned the case over to the intelligence division. We ended by socking the professor with a hefty bill for back taxes, plus 6% annual interest, plus a 50% penalty. I hope he learned that if he wanted to make a hobby of needling government agencies he should pick his opponents more carefully.

Stockbrokers have the same privacy problems as banks. There is no federal law explicitly requiring either a banker or a broker to keep customers' records secret. There are state laws requiring the police and other prowlers to obtain search warrants under certain conditions, and there are rules of evidence that the prowler must observe if he anticipates that the case he is working on will end in a court. But a revenue agent or special agent does not find these rules very burdensome. The vast bulk of tax cases are settled out of court. We simply show the TP what information we have on him, overwhelm him with it, convince him he can't hope to put up an effective fight. Most taxpayers back down quickly. Since so few of our cases get to court, we aren't that much concerned about search warrants or rules of evidence or other items of police etiquette. If a revenue agent wants information, he simply walks in and asks for it.

I recall auditing an immoderately rich man whose stock-market manipulations troubled me. I don't know exactly what triggered my suspicions, but that subconscious warning buzzer I mentioned earlier was almost audible. I became convinced, without having any evidence to support the notion at first, that the rich TP was playing a large number of Wall Street games that did not show up on his tax returns. I was sure he maintained accounts in at least two brokerages: an overt account whose records he showed me openly, plus at least one secret account.

I was conducting part of the audit in his office. He and his tax accountant and I were sitting arround his desk as this suspicion grew inside me. As I fidgeted in my chair, wondering how to approach the problem, I noticed a calendar on the wall. It was one of those promotional calendars that businesses give to clients and prospects. It bore the name of a brokerage house—not the one whose buy and sell slips the taxpayer had been showing me. I pretended to admire the calendar and asked the TP about it. He said airily that the brokerage had been trying to get his business, but since he already had a perfectly good broker he had seen no reason to switch his account. I nodded and let the matter drop.

I called on the local branch office of the brokerage whose name appeared on the calendar. The first person I talked to was a young man who seemed very worried about giving out information about the customers. "We can't do that!" he kept saying. "It's a violation of trust!"

Trust? A frail concept. The young man passed the

buck up to his boss, the branch manager, a woman of great grace and charm. She asked me to have a seat in her office. After I had waited there for about five minutes, she came in with a sheaf of paper. She handed it to me, smiling.

"Here are the records on your man for the past three years," she said. "If you want to go back farther than that, the main office in New York will help you. I just phoned them and they instructed me to give you whatever you need. If you'll follow me, there's an empty office down the hall that you can use. And would you like a cup of coffee?"

You see, dear TP, nothing is secret to me. Not even that most hallowed of all types of private data, your medical records. You probably hold the common and complacent belief that your doctor, bound by a strict code of ethics, will fight valiantly to protect the privacy of your relationship with him. He might fight such a fight if an ordinary cop or an FBI agent came snooping around after some piece of data. Assuming your doctor is a generally honorable citizen, he has nothing to fear from the local police department or the FBI. But let me stroll into his office waving my IRS credentials, and your doctor will in all likelihood melt like butter in a frying pan. He may go out of his way to be helpful, like the doctor who not only gave me the specific information I asked for but also offered, as a kind of goodwill bonus, to tell me about certain other wealthy patients whom he suspected of falsifying their medical tax deductions (provided I kept his name a secret, of course). Or he may argue for a while before he caves in. He may fear the patient's wrath nearly as much as he fears mine, in which case he and I may strike a bargain: In return for his giving me the data I want, I promise not to reveal that he is the source.

Such a bargain can get quite elaborate. I recall one case in which an advertising executive claimed a $6,000 deduction for what he called charitable donations to a tax-exempt nursing home. He showed me canceled checks to prove he had actually paid the home $6,000 during the year, but several clues led me to suspect these were not charitable donations. I suspected, instead, that the TP was keeping a relative in the home, perhaps his mother, and that the $6,000 represented the cost of room, board and nursing care for the patient. If this were so, the $6,000 would not be fully tax-deductible and might not be deductible at all. The rules say you can deduct sanitarium costs as a medical expense only if the patient is being treated for a specified ailment, and only if the same care can't readily be given at home. You can't deduct sanitarium costs if they simply reflect general care of an invalid.

I went to the nursing home to find out whether the TP had a relative there.

The doctor who operated the home very nearly genuflected before me. He wanted no trouble with IRS.

"I'll tell you the facts," he said. "We've got the man's mother here. This woman is nuttier than a fruitcake. Probably incurable. We give her no medical treatment. A couple of pills now and then; that's the extent of it. You've got a good case against the taxpayer. But listen, he mustn't ever find out I told you so. When he first put his mother in here he made a big deal out of privacy. He wanted to be sure all our records stayed locked up tight. I'll give you what you want, but it has got to look as though you got the stuff from somebody else, not me."

He asked me to sit tight for a few days while he mulled over the problem. A week later I received in the mail a sheaf of photocopies of bills sent to the adman by the nursing home. They were itemized bills, showing exactly what the nursing home had and had not done for the man's mother. A squeal letter was attached to the sheaf. It said: "I am an employee of the ———— Nursing Home. I have chanced to learn that you are seeking certain information regarding one of our patients. Being a patriotic citizen, I consider it my duty to help stamp out the evil of tax dodging. I enclose herewith the information you were seeking."

The letter was signed, "Honest Taxpayer."

Evidence gathered by devious means such as this can be shot down in court. That is one of the main reasons why all revenue agents and special agents are instructed to settle cases out of court whenever they can. In the normal run of cases this isn't at all hard to do. We are schooled in the art of demoralizing a TP, beating him down with evidence until he becomes convinced he can only make things worse by struggling. We don't tell him, of course, that the U.S. Attorney won't prosecute a weak or badly substantiated case. Our object is to convince the TP that the case against him is airtight, and our hope is that he will fold up without a fight. (His lawyer and accountant may play another version of the same game with him. They know a weak case when they see it, but they try to convince the poor old TP he is headed for a colossal penalty and 60 years in jail. When IRS peaceably settles the case out of court with no penalty, the lawyer and accountant mop their brows dramatically. "Wow, what a fight that was!" they say. Shortly afterward they clobber their double-conned client with two immoderately large bills.)

Most IRS agents, in their attempt to demoralize a TP

and keep him out of court, go at him as gently as they can. Some of us even do it with sympathy. But we do it doggedly nonetheless. Our job security and promotions depend mainly on the number of cases we settle and the amount of new tax money we bring in. No good agent, when he can help it, ever lets a taxpayer believe escape is possible via the court route. For every tax case that ends in court, thousands are settled by the taxpayer's voluntary capitulation.

It isn't an uncommon experience for an agent to work up a case that he *knows* will be shot down if he lets it get to court. Special agents of IRS have been known to tap people's phones, for example, or to bug taxpayers' homes and offices with secret listening devices, or to open people's mail through working agreements with local postmasters. One agent, testifying in a court case in the late 1960s, even went so far as to say he had been to a special IRS school that included wiretapping and other such espionage procedures in its curriculum. I have no firsthand knowledge that such a school exists, though I've heard it mentioned more than once. But I do know for certain that IRS agents routinely use spy techniques that most courts would consider unwarranted invasions of privacy. Such techniques work well for us because we don't go to court that often.

An agent using an illegal technique nurses two hopes: The first—the most common outcome—is that the taxpayer won't know enough about the law and, presented with the evidence against him, will instantly collapse. The second hope is that, even if the TP suspects he might put up a good fight in court, he won't be sure enough of his ground and thus will be amenable to a bargain.

IRS does a lot of bargaining with taxpayers in the

effort to stay out of court. In one of my own cases, I was poking through a taxpayer's records in a bank when I happened to see a pile of U.S. Treasury bonds on one of the bankers' desks. By sheer chance the bonds bore the name of another taxpayer whom I was in the process of auditing. The total value of the bonds was something like $150,000, an amount that was not consistent with the man's financial situation as reflected in his tax returns. Suspecting tax fraud, I turned the matter over to our intelligence division.

The special agent who worked on the case had a strong and uncomfortable feeling that the evidence of the bonds would not be admissible in court; I had had no good reason to pry into the taxpayer's private affairs—no "probable cause," in the legal phrase. The taxpayer himself realized this and he began to talk about hiring a lawyer and going to court. So we offered him a bargain. If he would capitulate and pay the back taxes we said were due, we would forget about any fraud penalty. But if he forced us into court, we would ask the U.S. Attorney not only to clobber him with a fine but also to press for a jail term.

As usually happens, the TP saw it our way. Alone against the might of the U.S. government, he lost his nerve. The case, which we would probably have lost, never got to court.

The Internal Revenue Service obviously has a lot of power to push defenseless people around. It probably has, in the aggregate, more such power over more people than any other government agency in the United States. Such power can be abused. In defense of my esteemed employer I must say that I don't believe the power is abused often. IRS is aware of the potential problem, is anxious to prevent a public outcry and watches its agents to make sure they don't swing their weight too carelessly. If a taxpayer writes in to complain he has been bullied or treated unfairly, that complaint is usually treated as a serious matter. The agent who did the alleged bullying is likely to be invited into his superior's office for a sharp lecture on public relations. He may also receive a call from IRS's internal police force, the feared inspection service. If there are more than a few taxpayer complaints about any one agent in one year, that agent will probably be taken out of the field and assigned to other duties. Even without this internal policing setup, the fact would still remain that most IRS agents, like most people in any other line of work, are fundamentally humane and therefore sympathetic to other people's problems.

But, unavoidably, there are agents who enjoy their power too much. Revenue officials and even U.S. presidents have sought to explain this problem away by reference to the statistical or "bad apple" theory of wrongdoing among civil servants. The theory is that there are bound to be x number of bad apples in every basket, and since this is an immutable law of nature there is nothing we can do about it. But it seems to me this approaches the problem upside down. Power corrupts. It doesn't corrupt everybody, but if it corrupts some, it is too much power. Instead of shrugging over bad apples, we ought to build checks and balances into the system so as to reduce the power.

Only rarely in the 60-year history of the U.S. income tax has any public group seriously examined the degree of power granted to IRS agents. It last happened in the mid-1960s. The Senate Judiciary Subcommittee on Admistrative Practice and Procedure held hearings on the topic and listened to so many horror stories about IRS agents' snooping and bullying tactics that the subcommittee chairman was moved to compare IRS to "a Gestapo preying upon defenseless citizens." A few newspaper and magazine stories reported the results of the hearings, and then the subject faded from the headlines and disappeared. Nothing was done to diminish IRS's power or to give citizens weapons against the Gestapo personalities in IRS's ranks, and the Revenue Service today is the same as it has always been: much too powerful for its own or the country's good.

The senators on the subcommittee heard taxpayers testify that IRS special agents casually open personal mail, tap telephones, pick locks, search homes and offices, all without warrants or other legal authority. They heard about the standard squeeze technique: To make taxpayer A give damaging information about taxpayer B, you threaten A with an audit. One special agent testified that he routinely broke state laws dealing with the ways in which evidence is supposed to be gathered. Many taxpayers told of being hounded mercilessly over taxes they didn't believe they owed. "With IRS you're guilty until you prove yourself innocent," one woman said. She reported that revenue officers had seized her bank account without giving her any chance to argue her case in a court. After going through a period of desperate trouble in which she had no money to pay current bills, she finally managed to prove she had paid the taxes IRS claimed she hadn't paid. Her payment, it turned out, had been lost through some kind of clerical error at the IRS regional office. The revenue men finally returned her bank account to her, but the damage had been done—she had been punished without a trial.

This peculiar outside-the-law status of IRS was

brought up often at the hearings. It was pointed out that an ordinary cop or FBI man working on a criminal case must observe all the rules with care because he knows the case *must* end in a court if it is ever going to be concluded at all. If he breaks the rules, he risks losing his case. But an IRS agent can operate more freely. He hopes the case won't go to court, and the statistical odds grossly favor him in this hope. He can make up his own rules as he goes along.

In my time at IRS I've met more than one agent who abused this enormous power. One special agent told me with evident pride of a technique he had used to get the goods on a businessman he suspected of tax evasion. He approached the man's secretary and asked her to send him photocopies of the businessman's private mail. When she balked he told her she could be subjected to a long jail term for "refusal to cooperate with a federal officer." This was sheer fiction, but it was enough to worry the girl. She did what he asked. Confronted with evidence gathered this way, the businessman meekly settled out of court. He paid his back taxes and a civil fraud penalty, and then he fired the girl.

In another case that makes me less than proud to be a revenue man, two agents called at the home of an elderly building-supplies dealer and interrogated him, not gently, for four straight hours. Their main quarry in that particular investigation was a large real-estate-development corporation, and they were trying to build their case by squeezing admissions of wrongdoing out of small businessmen who dealt with the corporation. They suspected that several building-supplies dealers were involved in schemes by which the corporation evaded taxes on a grand scale. In one scheme, dealers billed the corporation for supplies that were not delivered. The corporation paid the bills by check, and the dealers cashed the checks and returned the cash to the corporation. At tax time the corporation used the canceled checks as proof of a deductible business expense.

At any rate, the two agents harried the elderly dealer for an entire afternoon without even letting him get a drink of water. They went over and over his tax returns for several years back, magnified small errors and irregularities, threatened him with fines and jail. They forbade him to phone either his accountant or his lawyer, which is a citizen's right when cornered by an ordinary policeman. And of course they failed to observe other rules of police etiquette: They neither warned the man against self-incrimination nor told him it was his right to remain silent if he wished. (An IRS agent is supposed to advise a TP of his rights whenever a case appears to be turning into a criminal investigation, but in practice the agent generally waits to utter the required warning until after he has gathered the data he wants. If he is challenged about this later, he simply says he didn't realize at first that his case was becoming a criminal matter. The point at which a civil case metamorphoses into a criminal one is nearly impossible to spot precisely.)

Toward the end of the afternoon, slumping with fatigue and literally in tears, the old dealer was still denying any involvement in tax conspiracies with the corporation. But to get the agents' teeth out of him he began blurting out admissions of minor tax dodges of his own. They were the kinds of dodges that nearly every taxpayer uses: He had overstated a medical expense here and there, had failed to report a few hundred dollars of cash income, and so on. The agents pounced on these little transgressions and used them as a lever against him. They threatened him with seizure of his bank account and other property, and finally they made him agree to be their spy for the next several weeks. Carrying a concealed recording device, he was to roam around the local building industry and engage people in private conversations about tax schemes.

The agents got the dirt they were looking for. More than a dozen local businessmen were caught in the roundup —none of which took place in a courtroom. When word got around that the old building-supplies dealer was IRS's undercover man, his business suffered so badly that he had to close it down. Deep in debt, he sold his home at a loss and crawled out of town.

The revenue officers of our collection division—the guys who go out and physically grab money from TPs who haven't paid up—enjoy a different kind of power. Not only are they empowered to spy on people in the course of hunting for hidden wealth, but they can seize people's property without going through any court procedures. This power of seizure can be even more dangerous in the wrong hands than the power to spy and harass.

If IRS believes you owe money that you haven't paid, a revenue officer will be assigned to squeeze you. He will usually begin with a series of dunning letters or phone calls or both. If these yield no juice, he makes out a special levy form that gives him the right to seize your bank account, your car, your house, your stocks or any other salable property. He makes out this form all by himself, with no judge or anybody else to make sure he handles the affair properly. If the amount of money involved is unusually large, he may get his superior to sign the levy. Otherwise he is on his own. He can walk into your bank, wave the levy at a bank officer and demand that your money be handed over to him. The bank officer will have no practical choice but to obey.

I was a revenue officer in the beginning of my IRS career and I didn't enjoy it. Many TPs I dealt with were down to their last few bucks. I tried to be kind. I fifty-threed a lot of tax debts (declared them uncollectable), and I leaned over backward to help troubled folks out of their money difficulties. Most revenue officers do. But there are some who pride themselves on rarely fifty-three-ing anybody, no matter how bad the TP's money position may be. I've known revenue officers who hounded people into circumstances of near starvation. One officer of my acquaintance even hounded a poor fellow who was in the hospital recuperating from the long illness that had caused his tax delinquency and other financial troubles. The officer finally fifty-threed the case when the TP died.

It isn't hard to find bad apples in a big basket like IRS, of course. I'm not trying to say the percentage of Gestapo types in IRS is greater than in any other government agency. I'm not even registering a complaint about the existence of Gestapo types. Such a complaint would be useless. People are people. I am saying only that given the existence of Gestapo mentalities it seems foolish and dangerous to leave power lying around where they can grab it. I even feel it is dangerous to give *me* such power, though I fondly consider myself to be a man of moderation and—well, a nice guy. I don't beat my wife; I take my children to zoos and buy them ice-cream cones; I get along amicably with my suburban neighbors; and I have never used any more than the minimum necessary force to make a taxpayer see things my way. Yet my power scares me sometimes. If I can get at privileged information such as a doctor's private files, if I can find out almost anything about any citizen without getting permission from a judge or seeing the inside of a courtroom, what am I? I am a small-sized version of George Orwell's Big Brother—the eye to which all walls are glass.

Chapter 10

A SOFTHEARTED GESTAPO, ANYWAY

The remarks I have just made need to be put in their proper perspective. Although the Internal Revenue Service is probably the world's most powerful police agency, the fact is that it often shrinks from using its power aggressively. It makes full use of its virtually unrestricted license to spy on people. But when it catches them doing wrong it often treats them with a gentleness that has amazed many. It is a shy and softhearted giant. It could crush people underfoot if it wanted to. Sometimes it does. Usually it doesn't. I still think it is dangerous to have such a giant on the loose. The giant could conceivably go berserk. But it must be reported that so far IRS has used its enormous power with great moderation.

We revenue folks like to throw our weight around a little during the first quarter of the year, from January through March. The object is to achieve a climax of fraud convictions in late March and early April. We want these convictions to be widely reported in the newspapers. We want every taxpayer to be a little scared while making out his return in the dark night of April 14. The rest of the year we hang our big stick in the closet and walk softly.

The most celebrated example of our gentleness was the case of Joe Louis. Maybe you remember poor old Joe. *Ebony* magazine, on the occasion of a party that was recently organized in Detroit to raise money for Joe, grumbled about his unkind treatment at the hands of an oppressive United States government. I find the notion unlikely. Not only unlikely, but almost weird in its topsy-turvy assessment of the facts. *Ebony* may have been referring to Joe's troubles in the 1960s over a business venture in Cuba, but if the magazine meant to include IRS in its grumpy remarks, I am baffled. The fact is that the Brown Bomber earned income on which he failed to pay the proper tax. The mess was of his own making. IRS let him walk away.

The mad saga began on the night of June 22, 1937, when the 23-year-old Joe Louis beat James J. Braddock in Chicago and became world heavyweight boxing champion. He held the crown for 12 years, during which time he won 68 fights, 54 of them by knockouts. He retired on March 1, 1949, two weeks before his 1948 tax return was due.

During that brilliant 12-year career, Taxpayer Louis earned a lot of dollars. The coaching and advice he got in the ring were obviously first-rate, but the financial counseling he received was not. He did not put enough aside to pay income taxes. Pay-as-you-go taxation was only instituted in the early 1940s and it didn't begin to work properly until about 1950. Throughout the span of

Louis's career in the ring, a man whose income was in a form other than wages or a salary could easily get into the bind of forgetting about his tax liability. He could go all year without paying any tax, and then suddenly March 15 (the due date in those years) would be upon him. He would discover that he owed more tax than his cash position could cover.

Louis spent his money freely, often with notable generosity. He handed out hundred-dollar tips with gay abandon. He gave thousands of dollars to friends and relatives in needy circumstances. Each March he found himself short of the cash needed to pay IRS (then known as BIR). He paid some tax, but not enough. His deficiency mounted year by year.

BIR men called on him from time to time. They would point out that he owed such-and-such from prior years, plus still more for this year, and ask when he meant to pay. Louis would reply, "Next big purse." But the next big purse always seemed to be empty by the time the BIR men came around again.

It has been said by some that BIR was much too easy-going in those early years; that more strictness would have been a greater kindness in the long run. Perhaps so. If BIR had garnisheed some of the Brown Bomber's prize purses in the beginning and wiped out his debt and restarted him with a clean slate, everything might have gone more smoothly. The trouble was no BIR official wanted to take the responsibility of cracking down that way on so well-liked a popular hero. And so Louis's total tax deficiency mounted.

By 1960 it seemed unlikely to Internal Revenue Commissioner Dana Latham that Louis could ever erase his debt. "His earning days are over," Latham told the House

Appropriations Subcommittee in 1960 when he was asked what IRS proposed to do about Louis. The aging fighter was in fact nearly broke by this time. He had earned but little money since he left the ring in 1949. At various times through the 1950s he had paid certain sums toward the tax debt, but the interest was compounding inexorably. He was like Jack trying to climb a beanstalk that was growing faster at the top than he could shinny up from the bottom. "His situation is hopeless," said Latham.

And so the kindly IRS accepted an offer in compromise from Louis's lawyer. In June 1960 much of the fighter's debt to the United States government was simply forgiven.

Many taxpayers reacted with ferocious anger. Some of the anger was evidently motivated by racism: the feeling among some white groups that the government was leaning too far backward to be good to a black man. But most TPs were angry just because they felt Louis should have been made to pay his share.

"This man lived high for twelve years," one embittered TP wrote to Latham, "while I was forced to deny myself luxuries in order to pay my proper tax. I must now ask myself whether I was a fool. . . ."

Replying to such criticism in Congress, Dana Latham said, "We got all we could reasonably expect from Mr. Louis, leaving him with some hope that he can live." Latham was saying, in other words, that IRS had been motivated by practicalities (mainly the blood-from-a-turnip question) and by ordinary human sympathy. Nothing could be gained, Latham felt, by trying to punish the Brown Bomber any more harshly than life had already punished him. Even if he could have been charged with a jailable offense and locked up (willful fraud would have been tough to prove in his case), the outcry might have been far louder than that over the compromise.

Sympathy and the turnip question—these are two common reasons why the Revenue Service often surprises people with its unwillingness to wield power. Another reason is sheer lack of manpower. It would take a million-man staff to follow through on every case of suspected or possible cheating. Indeed, it often happens that a certified cheat goes unpunished because nobody has time to pursue the case. I once caught a taxpayer red-handed playing the old refund game on a magnificent scale. To play this game, you start by overpaying certain deductible items. If you owe a doctor $50, for instance, you mail him a check for $150. When his nurse phones to tell you about your error, you say, "Oh, my, how stupid of me. Would you refund the difference?" The nurse sends you back $100. At tax time, you've got a canceled check to prove a $150 medical deduction.

The TP I caught doing this was a $60,000-a-year executive. His charity deductions looked abnormally high to me. Even though he had canceled checks to substantiate his claims, I heard that funny little buzzer in the back of my skull. I decided to spot-check a couple of the deductions and find out what was going on.

The first phone call I made was to the man's alma mater, a small midwestern college. He claimed to have donated $2,500 to the annual fund drive. I asked the college bursar to check his records and see whether the contribution was as claimed. It was not.

"I remember this because it was kind of screwy," the bursar told me. "The fellow mailed us a check for twenty-five hundred. Couple of weeks later he phoned me and said he'd run into an unexpected financial problem and would I mind sending him back two grand? Well, hell, what could I say? I sent him a check the next day."

I asked the bursar to send me a certified true photocopy of his canceled $2,000 check. He said he would.

I checked a couple of the taxpayer's other charitable donations in the same way and found the same game going on. Then I checked some of his medical deductions. Same story. Real-estate taxes? Same story. The TP had even played the refund game with a hospital-insurance company and with a bank that had loaned him money to buy a car. He had paid the insurance company two annual premiums instead of one and had received an automatic refund, and he had overpaid interest to the bank.

I was up against a clear case of willful fraud, eminently provable if IRS chose to take it to court. A taxpayer can make a couple of overpayment mistakes and get away with them, but when he does it a dozen times a court can easily be convinced he acted deliberately. I bucked the case to the intelligence division.

And intelligence bucked it back.

"They don't want it," my chief said. "They're up to the ears in work. There isn't a special agent within five hundred miles who's free to take on anything else."

"So what do you want me to do?" I asked.

The chief shrugged. "For now, just assess him for the deficiency and interest. Maybe intelligence will want to go after him later."

I audited three years of the man's returns and ended with a tax-and-interest liability of about $16,000. He paid with relief. As far as I know, intelligence never gave him a second glance. He never paid a penalty.

Because of our manpower shortage, and because of a similar shortage in the Justice Department (which prosecutes all the cases we want to steer into court), we vastly prefer to settle cases out of court when we can. We prefer it even though, as in the case of Joe Louis, we lose a lot of money by making compromises with taxpayers. Not only do careless nonpayers like Louis get away undertaxed, but so do deliberate nonfilers in many cases.

I remember one fellow who failed to file any tax returns at all for about seven years. The first year, he explained, he hadn't filed because he was broke. Like Joe Louis he simply didn't have the cash to pay his tax. The second year he had the cash but he was afraid to file. He didn't know how to answer that little question on the front of the 1040: Did you file last year, and if not, why not? The same problem recurred every year thereafter. He was finally caught when a computer saw his Social Security number turning up on some information returns but couldn't find the corresponding number on any tax return. Special agents determined that he owed something like $85,000 in taxes for the seven years. Interest and a fraud penalty would have made the amount considerably larger. But we settled for $30,000, to be paid over a three-year period. Why? Because in the circumstances it seemed like the most sensible thing to do. Consider our alternatives:

One alternative would have been to haul him into court and prosecute him for criminal fraud. We would probably have won the case. His lawyer proposed to argue that only his first year of nonfiling was blameworthy; that all the subsequent years' nonfilings were motivated by a fear of self-incrimination. This probably would not have stood up. Similar cases have been in the courts, and the courts have generally held that a willful failure to pay taxes cannot be excused just because the underlying motive was fear of IRS. As one judge remarked, this would be like excusing a bank robber for shooting a policeman while trying to get away. You can't justify a crime because its purpose was to help the criminal escape prosecution for another crime. Thus, the feeling in IRS was that we had a winning case if we wanted to go to court. But we didn't really want the taxpayer in jail. He was an executive of a large, rather conservative company. Officers of the company made it quite plain that they would summarily fire the man if he went to jail. If he was fired, his income would stop. He had a high income but little in the way of savings or investments. If we stopped his income, we would have small hope of ever seeing more than a fraction of the money he owed.

Another alternative would have been to assess a 50% civil-fraud penalty against him. Such a penalty can be assessed by IRS without going to court. The taxpayer can choose to pay it if he believes a court fight would be a worse alternative for him—if he believes, for example, that a U.S. Attorney will press for a high fine and a jail term. But he can also choose to fight the assessment in court. Our seven-year nonfiler and his lawyer indicated that they would fight. The taxpayer pointed out that he didn't have anything like the amount of money that would be needed to pay his tax deficiency plus 50%. He was prepared to go to jail if he had to. He knew we would have to take him to court if we wanted him in jail, and his lawyer probably guessed we didn't want him in jail.

Our only good alternative was to squeeze the man for whatever amount of money he could feasibly pay. His lawyer let drop the hint that if we squeezed too hard the man would go into bankruptcy, and then we'd never get a worthwhile payoff. So we compromised for $30,000.

It is the nature of the system that many probable and even certifiable cheats are deliberately allowed to slip away at the initial auditing stage. A revenue agent working against tax-money and case-closing quotas has no very strong motive to turn his audits into fraud cases. His chief wants him in the field producing, not tangled up in conferences with special agents and lawyers. If I catch a TP cheating, I greatly prefer to believe the cheating wasn't deliberate. For me, a successful audit is one that ends with the taxpayer signing a simple deficiency agreement. I will turn a case over to intelligence only when the cheating is so blatant that I can't justify any other approach. I often suspect willful fraud, but I seldom go out of my way to prove it.

In a typical case I may catch a man with a bundle of T&E deductions he can't back up. I know damned well most of the claimed expenses are fake and I may even find some way to prove deliberate fraud. But what's the use? My chief will be happier, I'll be happier, the taxpayer will be happier and the whole world will be happier if I simply disallow part of what he can't prove and let it go at that.

The philosophy of IRS is that getting the tax money comes first. Punishing delinquents is important only insofar as it frightens other would-be cheats and so brings in more tax money. We hold, in general, that punishment isn't worth the trouble unless there is a perceptible profit in it for the U.S. government. As in the case of the seven-year nonfiler, we almost always opt for money over vengeance. It is always better to collect part of what a man owes than to crush him and perhaps collect nothing.

We also subscribe to the old saying, "Better late than never." There are two ways to pay your taxes late: legally and illegally. But the difference is mainly technical. In practical terms—in terms of the taxpayer's treatment by IRS—the difference hardly exists. The treatment is likely to be the same in both cases: 6% annual interest, period.

The legal way to pay your taxes late begins with Form 4868. (There is a form for everything at IRS.) This form is essentially a request for a 60-day extension of time —meaning until June 15 for the majority of taxpayers who operate on a calendar-year basis. You don't have to give any reasons for filing a late return on a 4868 request. The extension is granted automatically.

Next comes another form: 2688. If you want an extension beyond June 15, you file this form and state your reasons. Almost any half-baked reason is likely to be accepted: You've been sick, or your accountant has been sick, or you've just learned of a new IRS rule that requires a recalculation of your figures. The only unacceptable reasons are that you don't have the money to pay your tax or you want to use the money temporarily for another purpose. These are nearly everybody's real reasons; just be careful not to say so on Form 2688.

A 2688 request will bring you an extension of up to six months. The law says that longer extensions will not be allowed "under any circumstances." Obviously this is mere bluster. As has been demonstrated in the case of Joe Louis and several million other cases, IRS is delighted to collect any tax even if it's more than 30 years late. As a matter of fact, IRS is delighted when it can collect the principal, let alone the interest.

A taxpayer who wants to pay later than the six months technically allowed by a 2688 request has several different approaches to choose from. He can, if he wishes, simply fail to pay. Revenue officers will begin to send him dunning letters after a while, but if he is lucky the collection division will be too busy to pay much attention to him for months. He may find he can stretch his extension to a year or more before a revenue officer comes around talking about attachments and garnishments.

Or, if it makes the tardy TP feel safer, he can use various tricks to demonstrate his intention to pay. Many taxpayers use such tricks on April 15, without even troubling to fill out 4868s. If it's April 15 and you don't feel like paying your tax right away, you can send us a check but forget to sign it. So many taxpayers do this that at some offices a man may be employed full time for weeks to do nothing but phone or write nonsigners. He may go down his list alphabetically, which means that you will get the longest unofficial extension if your name begins with Z.

In another fairly common ruse, a taxpayer deliberately neglects to mail his return on April 15. After a couple of months—whenever he is ready to pay the tax—he writes or phones his local IRS office. He says, "Say, aren't you folks ever going to cash my check?"

The lady on the phone says, "If it was received April fifteenth, it ought to have been processed by now."

The TP says, "My goodness, it hasn't come back through my bank yet. Do you suppose my return got lost?"

Lost returns are common enough at IRS, so we can't reasonably accuse this taxpayer of deliberately conning us. We can strongly suspect him of it, but we can't do much about our suspicions.

Lack of money is the most common reason for late filing. The second most common reason—having a better use for the money—is more interesting. In effect, a late-filing TP is borrowing money from IRS at a ridiculously low rate of interest.

A taxpayer might owe us $10,000, for example. He would like to have the use of $10,000 for half a year to pursue some private goal—perhaps to buy some stock that he believes will appreciate pleasantly over the next six months. Where else can he borrow money at 6%? Nowhere but dear old IRS. The benevolent Gestapo.

Chapter 11

THE
TAX
INFORMERS

I met my favorite tax informer on a hot August afternoon. He was a public accountant, and I had come to his office to go over the tax returns of a doctor, one of the accountant's clients. The office was small, densely cluttered and fearfully hot. I had my jacket off, my tie loosened, my sleeves rolled up. Nothing helped. Sweat rolled down my forehead. The only thing I wanted in the world was to finish the audit and get out. I wanted to find an air-conditioned bar and buy myself a cold, cold beer.

Accountancy firms often provide hot, stuffy offices for revenue agents to work in. The less comfortable the office, the shorter the audit is likely to be. Some big companies even reserve special Discomfort Rooms (DRs, my own private term) for visiting revenue men. The standard DR is about eight feet square. It has no windows. The temperature is some 60 degrees in the winter and 85 in the summer. The only source of light is a yellow 60-watt bulb, and the DR is situated directly under the stamping machine in the mailroom. But on this particular August afternoon I didn't believe I was in a specially designed DR of that type. The office was uncomfortable because it was all the accountant could afford.

The accountant was a small pale man, nearly bald, with a whispery voice. He wore a dark suit. His jacket was on, neatly buttoned. His tie was tight against his Adam's apple. The collar points of his white shirt, frayed but clean, curled up damply in the heat. Beads of sweat stood out on his pale, smooth head.

We were nearing the end of our work when the taxpayer himself dropped in. The doctor-TP was a large man with heavy black-rimmed glasses and a loud voice. He was suntanned. He wore yellow pants and a red sport shirt. I wasn't quite sure, but I thought he might be a little drunk. He said he had just finished a golf game and had stopped by to see how the audit was coming.

As it happened, there were a few unsubstantiated expense deductions that I had chosen to disallow. Nothing spectacular. In my hurry to get the hell out and wrap myself around a cold beer, I had leaned far in the taxpayer's favor. I'd given him the benefit of the doubt most of the way. There were some stock-market transactions that looked a little fishy to me, but I had even let these potential problems ride by. The last thing I wanted was a long wrangle. As we neared the end of the audit, it looked as though the doctor would come out in fair shape. His extra tax liability was a mere 300 bucks or so. Since his stated gross income was in the $30,000 range, I doubted this would hurt him much. But apparently it did.

"My God, Ackerman!" he yelled at the little accountant. "What the hell do I pay you for? To give my money
away?"

The accountant sat there silently and gazed down at
the papers on his desk. The doctor made some more acid
comments about the accountant's professional abilities,
browbeating him as though I wasn't there. I thought
maybe I should rise to the little man's defense, but I
couldn't think of anything useful to say. Even when the
accountant looked up at me once as though asking for
help, I took the cowardly way out. I just sat there.

The doctor's last words were particularly unkind, I
thought. "I don't know why the hell I hired you, Ackerman," he said. "I guess I felt sorry for you. This teaches
me a lesson, by God! I'll never again mix business and
sentimentality!"

He went out, slamming the door. I said, "Jeez, I'd
hate to be one of his patients. Is he like that all the time?"

Little Ackerman nodded sadly. "I've been living with
it for years. Sometimes I wonder . . ."

He stood up and went to the window, then beckoned
me over. The window looked down onto a small parking
lot. Ackerman and I watched the doctor walk to his car, a
gorgeous new white Cadillac.

Ackerman said, "His wife has a new Continental, and
each of his kids has a new Porsche."

I got the point, of course. I nodded, and recited a
little piece of private IRS doggerel: "You wonder how, on
thirty thou."

Ackerman shrugged and went back to his desk, apparently ready to let the matter drop. But I wasn't ready.
Maybe I was irritable because of the heat, or maybe I just
hate to see a little guy get picked on. Even revenue agents

have hearts. At any rate, for whatever reason, I was in a mood to deal the doctor a low kick. I did something field agents are not encouraged to do. I told Ackerman about our informer program.

The Internal Revenue Service does not actually invite citizens to inform on each other; "invite" is much too strong a word. It is more accurate to say that machinery exists quietly within IRS for processing tips from informers. We don't advertise it; we simply allow it to exist and let it go at that. Never, in my memory, has any revenue official deliberately publicized this machinery or urged citizens to use it. Quite the contrary, in fact. On the rare occasions when newspaper or magazine reporters come around and ask us about it, we say as little as we can. Somehow we don't like it. But there it sits.

The rewards range from 1% to 10% of the taxes and penalties collected as the result of a tip. The size of the reward depends on a recommendation by the special agent assigned to the case. He bases his recommendation on the completeness and general usefulness of the data supplied by the informer.

Ackerman listened quietly as I told him all this. I finished my business with him, left his office, hunted down my cold beer and forgot all about him.

He phoned me about six months later. He had the goods.

His detective work had been admirable. He had begun by assuming the doctor was hiding income—not an unreasonable assumption, but a very difficult one to prove. The problem was to obtain substantiation that the Revenue Service could use in court.

We have already seen that the average middle-income TP, who gets his income mainly from a single employer, has but little opportunity to hide income to any important extent. The W-2 form or Form 1099 that the employer is required by law to send IRS at the end of each year tells us the total wages or salary paid to that man or woman by that employer that year. And even though our computers don't cross-check all these forms against all tax returns, and admitting that a lot of forms get lost in our enormous year-end shuffle, the very existence of such forms is a strong deterrent against underreporting income. A taxpayer can hope his employer's W-2s or 1099s will get lost, but he can never assume they will.

Doctors and many other kinds of professionals, as I explained earlier, escape this problem. The mind-boggling task of checking the itemized medical deductions of the typical doctor's several hundred patients against his declared income, even with computers to help, is one that IRS doesn't often undertake. A doctor can thus safely assume we don't know precisely what his income is.

Ackerman, as an accountant and veteran tax preparer, knew these facts well. He asked himself two questions. One: Where and how can a man hide income? Two: Where would the evidence of this income be likely to surface?

He thought first of banks. As the doctor's accountant, Ackerman knew the bank with which the doctor did his principal business. The deposits made in this bank were quite consistent with the doctor's stated $30,000 gross income. Ackerman wondered: Might the doctor have another bank account in another town, where he secretly deposited income beyond his stated gross?

After mulling over this possibility for a while, the canny little accountant rejected it. He knew his client well. The doctor, Ackerman believed, was a man of more than ordinary greed. Such a man would not like to see his money lie idle; he would want to invest it, in the hope of making still more money with it. In a secret bank account he would have no such opportunity, for a secret account cannot be an interest-bearing account. You can keep a checking account secret from the Revenue Service (for a while, anyway), but a savings account is an open book. The law requires banks to tell us what interest you earn each year, and this reveals the existence of the account.

Ackerman strongly doubted the doctor would want to put his money in a checking account and simply let it sit. Where else might the money go? Ackerman's next thought was the winner: *the stock market.*

The doctor had been fascinated by the stock market ever since Ackerman had known him. Not only fascinated; obsessed. Ackerman knew the doctor's principal broker and was familiar, of course, with the transactions in that brokerage account. The doctor made little money in that account. Most years, his losses neatly canceled out his gains. Ackerman began to toy with an intriguing notion. The more he thought about it, the more he liked it. Might it be, he wondered, that the doctor maintained a second account at another brokerage?

You can deposit money into a brokerage account as into a bank account. If you score capital gains, the brokerage is under no obligation to report them to IRS. There is a reporting requirement if you buy stocks that pay dividends. But if you carefully stick with zero-dividend securities—of which there are thousands traded over the counter as well as on the major exchanges—the existence of your account isn't likely to be revealed to us at Revenue, at least not in the normal course of events.

Ackerman now asked himself how he could find the

doctor's second account, if it existed. His solution was simple and direct. He belonged to a fraternal organization in his town, and one of the other members was the mailman whose delivery route included the doctor's home. The mailman, as Ackerman learned to his delight, didn't like the doctor much, evidently because of some long-standing quarrel about a lost package that the doctor believed to have been stolen. Ackerman bought the mailman a couple of drinks and made a proposition whose exact nature I don't know and don't want to know. Whether through motives of revenge or for a cut in the reward money, or both, the mailman agreed to tell Ackerman the names of brokerage houses from whom the doctor received mail.

It turned out, as Ackerman had suspected and hoped, that the doctor received letters regularly from two brokerages. One was the house Ackerman and IRS knew about, the one where the doctor kept his open and declared account. The other was a smaller brokerage that Ackerman had never heard of.

The next part of the story is obscure to me, a fact with which I am well content. Somehow Ackerman obtained photocopies of four monthly account statements from this smaller brokerage. It is reasonable to suspect he and the mailman obtained these copies simply by opening envelopes addressed to the doctor by the brokerage. The two conspirators may have copied the account statements at night, carefully resealed the envelopes and delivered them a day later. This procedure is of course illegal. Not even the Revenue Service, which recognizes few restrictions on its prying license, is supposed to open citizens' first-class mail. (Revenue agents sometimes do, but technically that is against the rules.) For this reason neither I nor any other IRS agent involved in the case ever asked Ackerman how he got those four photocopies. The less we knew about that, the happier we suspected we'd be.

The account statements contained the doctor's doom. The first thing Ackerman noticed on studying them was that the doctor loved wash sales. If he had a stock whose market price was down since he bought it, he would sell the stock in his open, declared account. Thus he would establish a capital loss for tax purposes. But if he believed the stock's price dip was only temporary, he would simultaneously buy an equal number of shares in his secret account. This is a wash sale, and it doesn't wash with us at Revenue. The rules say that if you want to establish a deductible loss you may not buy back into the same stock for 30 days after you've sold it.

Another thing Ackerman noticed, with mounting pleasure, was that the doctor seemed to be a rapid trader in his secret account. He moved in and out of stocks very frequently, taking short- rather than long-term gains. A short-term gain, remember, is taxable as ordinary income.

Still another thing that met Ackerman's delighted gaze was the sheer size of this secret account. The doctor had about $200,000 worth of cash and stocks in it. Judging by the four-month record in Ackerman's hands, the doctor appeared to be deposting several thousand dollars of new cash in the account every month.

The upshot of the story is that we nailed the doctor and nailed him tight. I turned the matter over to the intelligence division, and a special agent went down to the brokerage and dug back through years of records. (In cases of suspected civil fraud there is no statute of limitations.) We ended by assessing the doctor for something over $130,000 in taxes, interest and penalties. We recommended the maximum allowable reward for Ackerman, and not long afterward he received a Treasury check for some $13,000.

If this story whets your appetite, fine. You are in the minority, but you are not alone. In an average year the various district and field offices of IRS hear from some 10,000 tipsters who want rewards. Normally, one in every five or six claims is approved. The rewards total about $1.5 million each year, and IRS collects $35 million or so in additional taxes, interest and penalties from those informed upon. It is not a large program when measured against Revenue's other colossal statistics. Not large, for example, when compared with the total yearly tax takes, which are now running close to $200 billion. But the program does exist, and if you want to take advantage of it, we will lend an interested ear to your story.

The procedure is simple. If you have a story to tell, merely write or phone the intelligence division at the IRS district office where you pay your taxes. If your story seems sound, a special agent will be assigned to follow it up. If he finds your allegations to be provably true, you will be asked to fill out and sign something called an Application and Public Voucher for Reward for Original Information, otherwise known as Form 211. This application will meander its way through a series of organizational procedures, in the course of which various agents and officials will sign it and attach copies of other forms to it. If the untidy clump of paper doesn't get lost under more paper in somebody's out box, in the end you'll receive either a check or a sad letter saying your application has been denied.

To win any reward money at all—indeed, to get anybody at IRS even remotely interested—you must come up with solid and specific information. Mere suspicions are not enough; nor is hearsay. Each April every revenue office receives a steady flow of purported tips that are really nothing more than unfounded accusations—from disgruntled citizens in some cases, from outright nuts in others. Some of the accusations might be accurate for all we know. But our manpower is in short supply, and we won't risk agents' time unless there is a reasonable chance of a payoff.

One elderly lady, for example, apparently has it in for a wealthy real-estate tract developer in her hometown. Every year her local revenue office gets a letter from her, charging him not only with tax-dodging but also with moral turpitude and other failings. As proof she once submitted a newspaper photograph of the man and called attention to his "vulpine face."

At another office where I worked we got a letter from a college student of leftist persuasion. He included a membership list of an expensive country club near his home. "It is common knowledge that 90% of these business executives cheat on their taxes," he wrote. "Their moral caliber is uniformly low."

In presidential-election years we receive letters suggesting we probe the tax behavior of the major candidates.

None of this is much help to IRS, of course. What we buy, when we buy anything, is hard fact. Often it takes a good deal of work to develop the kind of fact that wins reward money—so much work, indeed, that you sometimes wonder what drove the man to do it.

In one case a waiter in a high-priced restaurant became curious about certain actions of the owner. Each night after the restaurant closed the owner would remove the tape from the cash register and put it in his pocket.

He would then throw out all the waiters' checks. At the end of each week he would give the bookkeeper a plain piece of paper on which he had written the alleged total of the week's gross receipts.

The waiter asked himself why the owner didn't simply hand the bookkeeper the cash-register tapes. He thought he knew the answer, and his suspicions were confirmed at the end of one particularly busy week. The bookkeeper looked at the week's alleged gross receipts and remarked to the owner, "Slow week, huh?" The owner nodded sadly.

The waiter now began a project that took him an entire year. He arrived at the restaurant early each morning, before the local sanitation company came around to collect the trash. He grubbed the waiters' checks out of the trash and took them home. At the end of a year he had a large box full of them. He laboriously added them up and thus arrived at a calculation of the restaurant's true gross. He mailed this information, along with the box of checks, to the Revenue Service.

The reward he finally received for this year of labor was about $200.

Tax-informing has been lucrative for some, but not for others. It is a risky business at best: You seldom know what the payoff will be, if any, and it is also the kind of business that can make enemies for you. The Revenue Service will scrupulously keep your identity a secret if you so request, but it is altogether likely that the taxpayer you inform on will guess who you are before the case is concluded. Is the game worth the prize?

I've already said that IRS has ambivalent feelings about the whole program. You will never see a discreet little advertisement on your Form 1040 that says, "Need cash to pay your tax? Ask about our special Rat Program." Indeed, we have become more and more silent about the program in the changing political climate of recent years. Particularly among younger taxpayers there has been a growing distrust of government authority and an accompanying exaltation of the private citizen and his rights. The Revenue Service, whose mandated assignment is to invade citizens' privacy on a massive scale, is highly nervous about this shift in attitude. Informers draw little praise in such a climate, and government agencies that use informers are accused of harboring sinister, Gestapo-like motives. Thus our embarrassment about the program is growing more acute. Back in the 1950s IRS published detailed statistics on the subject, and there were passing references to it in the commissioners' annual reports. You will search in vain for any such reference in the 1970 or 1971 report.

I must point out that nearly every law-enforcement agency uses informers—a statement that has probably been true since the first tribal laws were enacted at the dawn of human history. But it is undeniably true, too, that the idea of squealing on a fellow citizen has never been particularly appealing to Americans. Even back in the 1950s, when the government's ends were nearly always assumed to justify its means, there were people at Revenue who found the informer program distasteful. Notable among them was Commissioner T. Coleman Andrews, who ran IRS from 1953 to 1955. After leaving office Andrews made it plain that he hadn't enjoyed his job much and was unhappy with the entire American tax-collecting system. "I did not like the informer program any more than I liked the evils of the income tax itself," Andrews wrote to a reporter in 1959. "I hold that any tax system is funda-

mentally unsound that cannot be enforced without en-
couraging people to be stool pigeons."

What makes people inform on each other? The most
obvious motive is the reward money, but it is by no means
the most common motive. At least nine out of ten tax informers fail to ask for any reward at all (and since they
don't ask for it, we don't pay it). Some are motivated by
a desire for personal revenge, like Ackerman the accountant. Some are motivated by patriotism; they are angry because the nation's laws are being broken or because they
feel the nation needs more tax money to grow stronger.
But in my experience and that of other agents I've talked
to, by far the most common motive is plain jealousy. The
archetypical informer is a fellow of modest means, a wage
or salary earner who has little opportunity to do any tax-
cheating of his own. He discovers that somebody richer
than himself is getting away with a bundle of Uncle Sam's
money, and it makes him so mad that he sqeals.

Typically, he discovers the fat cat's dishonesty by ac-
cident—by just happening to be in the right place at the
right time. One such informer was a church minister who
chanced one Monday morning to visit a bank far from his
hometown. He saw a member of his congregation, a store
owner, standing at a teller's window and depositing rolls
of nickels, dimes and quarters.

This puzzled the minister. Several years ago the store
owner had approached him after a church service and
asked how much cash turned up in the average Sunday
collection. The minister had replied that it was usually
in the range of 50 to a hundred dollars. The store owner
had said, "Great! I need a lot of small change in my business. From now on, let me buy it from you every Sunday.
You give me the change, I'll give you a check."

The minister was happy to go along with the suggestion, for he was worried about a rising tide of Sunday collection robberies. But now, several years later, it turned out that the store owner didn't really want the small change after all. He was depositing it in a bank on a Monday morning. Why?

After mulling over the question for a few days, the minister called IRS. Since I had audited the store owner's return a couple of years back, I was called in on the case. I recalled that during the audit I had been surprised at the store owner's unusually generous contributions to his church. I had questioned him about them, but he had produced all his canceled checks to prove his case. Despite a nagging feeling of discontent about the situation, I had had to allow this TP a huge charity deduction.

We hit him for about $3,000 in back taxes, plus interest and a 50% civil-fraud penalty. The minister used part of his reward money to buy a safe for his church's Sunday cash.

In another case of revelation at a bank, an underpaid young engineer happened to notice the president of his company at a teller's window. What puzzled the engineer was that the president was apparently at the wrong window. The bank was a large one, and depositors' accounts were segregated alphabetically. If your name began with *A* to *E* you went to one teller; another teller handled *F* to *J*, and so on. The company president was evidently confused about his own name.

Or perhaps, the engineer thought later, he wasn't confused at all. This thought led to an investigation which eventually disclosed that the president had five different financial aliases by which he hid income. Revenue agents had to do most of the work on this case, and the young engineer got the minimum reward of 1%. But since the taxes and penalties added up to more than a million dollars, the reward was more than a token.

There have been several cases in which men, perhaps dissatisfied with the service received, have informed on prostitutes. Anytime a man meets a prostitute, from the lowliest streetwalker to the highest-priced call girl, he can fairly safely assume she is not declaring her income openly to the Revenue Service. A few prostitutes do file tax returns regularly, but most of these honest TPs still feel it's necessary to lie about their occupation. I have heard of at least one lady in the profession, however, who frankly wrote "prostitute" in the space where Form 1040 asks how you make your living. (To IRS, income is income no matter how earned. Since prostitution is not a federal offense, we would treat such a return no differently from that of a plumber.) However, since prostitutes get paid mainly in cash, and since the average customer can be counted on to keep the facts to himself, most women in the profession simply fail to file any tax returns at all. The percentage who get away with it must be in the nineties. But once in a while a man's wish to keep his sexual affairs private gets overwhelmed by his anger over a call girl's tax-free wealth. "What got me," one such informer explained to a special agent, "was the size of this girl's apartment. Twice as big as anything I'll ever have. When I thought what she was getting away with, it made me so mad that I left without— well, finishing." Over the next few weeks he did some amateur gumshoe work, bribed a bank employee to give him some facts about the girl's account and finally came to us.

A man who wanted to make a regular living out of tax-squealing might be able to do it by concentrating on high-priced call girls. Even then his income would be highly uncertain, and the fact is I've never heard of a regular tax informer or even a frequent repeater. As I've noted, the big killings in this business usually result from chance—from happening to hear or see something you weren't particularly looking for.

Still, there's probably no harm in staying alert. If you don't like your boss, or your divorced wife is giving you trouble, or your next-door neighbor irritates you, perhaps a little quiet sleuthing will lead you to some useful conclusions. Tax-informing, if you have the stomach for it, is certainly a handy form of revenge. And as Ackerman remarked to me after he received his Treasury check, "What could be better than to get revenge and get paid for it too?"

Well, it depends on your viewpoint. Before you get too excited about the possibilities, there is one last thing I ought to tell you. The reward you receive, if any, will not be as big as it seems. It will be taxable as income. And worse, it will almost guarantee you an audit.

Chapter 12

THE
TAX
AND
THE
SOCIETY

We have been talking about a lot of unpleasant subjects. Cheating. Bribery. Extortion. Informing. All these phenomena arise from the everyday workings of the income tax.

Back in 1894 a congressman warned that an income tax, if ever imposed in the United States, would "corrupt the people." Was he right? Have we all been corrupted?

I think it is important not to become unnecessarily dramatic in talking about this question. To say that an entire population has been "corrupted" would be not only fanciful but also impossible to prove. This is the kind of language that turns up in political speeches, college debates and rad-lib newspapers. As for us, let's keep cool and avoid exaggeration.

In the first place, we should recognize that what has

been happening to us has also been happening to the tax-payers of all other nations. If this is corruption, the whole world is going to hell in the same trolley car.

Second, we should recognize that the income tax is only one of many forces at work in our society. Any one of these forces can be singled out by an alarmist with a point to prove. The troubles that beset us can be blamed on almost anything: on the Vietnam War, on alcohol and/ or drugs, on urban sprawl, on "alienation" (whatever that is), on faulty child-raising practices, on the Republican or Democratic party, or on any other problem the alarmist happens to have on his mind, including the income tax.

With these cautions in mind, let's see what effect the income tax has on our society. Is it doing us harm?

I think so, and so do a lot of other people in and out of the Internal Revenue Service. I don't want to use the word "corruption" because that implies a moral judgment that I'm not prepared to make. I've remarked before that I can't blame taxpayers for cheating and, when I catch them doing it, I deliver no sermons. I prefer to think of avoidance and evasion—legal and illegal loopholing—as two variations of the same phenomenon. The phenomenon is tax-dodging. And what troubles me about it is not the morally corrupting effect, if any, but the enormous national waste of energy and good brainpower.

Norris O. Johnson, a New York banker, expressed the thought neatly a few years ago. "There has never been appeal to me," he said, "in the idea that, through its tax structure, our economy should be made to yield its richest rewards to the closest students of the tax laws."

The waste of human resources is huge. In an idealized capitalist society, an entrepreneur supposedly enriches everybody else while enriching himself. He puts his brain to work on the problem of making his company bigger and more productive, thereby creating new jobs and raising wages and making everybody happy. His motives are selfish, but the results are generally (with exceptions) beneficial to society.

Such a man was Henry Ford, for example. In the days before income taxes he showed the world a classic example of capitalistic self-interest working to improve a lightly taxed society. He spent his time figuring out how to make more cars more cheaply. He was able to raise wages at his plant while simultaneously dropping the prices of his cars. He didn't raise wages as fast as some union members wished, but at least he was heading in the right direction. Because taxation was not a major problem for him, he was free to spend his time and energy on the inventive improvement of his company.

In our present setup, man's inventive and creative energies are twisted in the wrong direction—call it corruption if you will. An inventive man must devote much of his brainpower to the problem of avoiding or evading taxes on his own or his company's income. This brings little benefit to the society.

I once audited a novelist who a couple of years back had produced a book that pleased both the critics and the buying public. It hadn't been a best seller, but it had been an undeniable artistic and financial success. The critics in their reviews said repeatedly that they hoped this man would turn out many more novels. They predicted a great future for him.

When I visited him, however, his future was stalled. He was taking at least a year off, not because he didn't want to write any more novels, but because his tax situation made idleness mandatory. He had rigged up a deal under which his publisher held money in escrow for him, paying it out at the rate of $35,000 a year instead of giving it to him all at once and pushing him into a confiscatory tax bracket. This $35,000 was all he needed and all he wanted in any one year. "There are several other novels I'd love to write," he told me, "but I can't do it. If my income goes any higher, you guys will take too much of it away from me."

It was society's loss as well as the novelist's. I went away from the audit wondering how many great books I will never read because tax problems kept them from being born. How many great plays and movies will never be produced for the same reasons? How many inventions don't exist because the inventors' energies were deflected into tax problems? How many potentially great companies are still scruffy little companies because human brainpower has been siphoned off by the tax? How big is the total loss of wealth, not only in money but in terms of an enriched culture?

The only visible benefit of this national attention to income taxation is that it provides employment for a vast herd of lawyers, accountants and tax experts who work full time to help citizens dodge the tax. Many of these experts are inexpert, and some are plain crooks, and it cannot be said that the society has lost a useful resource by having their energies deflected into the tax-dodging business. But others are impressively bright, and in their case the loss is incalculable. Imagine what might happen, for instance, if all the very clever people at H. & R. Block or the J. K. Lasser Tax Institute were to tackle some of society's important problems instead of spending their time helping other people reduce taxes.

"It seems dumb," a sage old CPA said to me once after

we had spent three days on one of his clients' returns. "IRS has 70,000 people to collect the tax, and there are hundreds of thousands of us other folks to keep you from doing your job too well. What's the point of it all? How does the country benefit from it?"

How indeed? The accounting profession likes to say it is in business as a kind of barrier against an overzealous IRS. This is a valid reason to be in business. No government agency should be allowed to operate without careful watchdogging and control by the public. Yet it seems sad to see the huge inventiveness of the accounting profession deflected into a task which in the end produces little to enrich the society.

I like to dream of a much simpler tax, perhaps not even a tax on income; a tax that wouldn't eat up so much useful energy in avoidance and evasion. I also like to dream of a better, more efficient, more cheatproof method of collecting the tax. I will discuss some of these thoughts in more detail in a later chapter—particularly the notion of the wonderful, but unfortunately theoretical, Diogenes Machine.

These are only dreams. Some of them may be realized in our lifetimes, but probably not until another few presidential elections have gone by. Until the needed improvements are made, each middle-income TP will have to swim or sink on his own. The chapters that follow contain swimming instructions.

PART III

YOU AND ME AGAINST THE TAX

*Wherein we see what a
solitary middle-income man
can do against the might of
the Internal Revenue Service.
And wherein we ask if better
and fairer taxation systems are
possible, and we end
optimistically by considering
the fabulous Diogenes
Machine.*

Chapter 13

HOW TO BE AUDITED AND COME OUT ALIVE

If your tax return is simple, the revenue man will probably do the job at his office and process you out in an hour or two. If it is complicated, he may come to your home or office and may take a whole day or longer. But the techniques of dealing with him, from your point of view, will be the same either way.

The objects of the game are 1) to finish the audit as fast as possible and 2) to make it end with the smallest possible assessment of additional tax for you (or, if you want to dream about the positive possibilities, the biggest possible refund). Obviously the basic determinant will be your tax return itself. But it will not be the only factor.

Auditing and being audited are in the realm of art, not science. If two different taxpayers filed exactly the same tax return and were audited by two different revenue men, the two results would almost certainly be different. They would be different because the personalities of the revenue man and the TP would be different in each case, and so would their interaction. The results could even be grossly dissimilar. One TP might go away with a refund, while the other ended in court defending a fraud charge.

I assume you would rather be the first taxpayer than the second. So I'm going to tell you how to get along with an office auditor or revenue agent. Thinking back over the long parade of taxpayers I've dealt with—the winners and the losers, the ones I liked and didn't like, the ones who irritated me, made me suspicious, made me vindictive—I think there are six important lessons for you to learn.

1. The Problem of Critical Distance

It is hardly necessary to point out that you don't want the auditing agent to be your enemy. On the other hand it is sheer damned foolishness to suggest (as some tax-advice columnists have) that you try to make him your friend. Gummy sentimentality like that will win you no points. What you must do is find the critical distance between you and him, neither too far nor too close. Failure to find that critical distance—an error in either direction—can land you in trouble.

Most taxpayers are smart enough to figure out that too much distance and coolness in the TP-agent relationship can lead to problems. Prekindergarten kids know that much about interpersonal relations. Of course I've handled many audits in which the taxpayer and I came to hate the sight of each other at the end, but the vast majority of taxpayers have at least had the good sense to start with a hopeful smile.

A few have been dumb enough to start by giving me

a kick instead of a smile. "Ah, it's the Gestapo," sneered one fellow when I turned up at his door. What he said may have been true, but there was no good reason to say it right then. Another man said sourly that he hoped the audit would be fast because he didn't like "wasting time with petty officials." Another dimwit, when his secretary offered me a cup of coffee, brusquely told her to forget it. "I don't want this guy here any longer than he has to be," he told her.

That kind of behavior is not only rude, but unprofitable. I'm as fair-minded as the next man, but I am a man, not a machine. If a taxpayer has started by making me dislike him, I will hardly be disposed to decide subjective or ambiguous questions in his favor. Many such questions come up even in a simple audit, and the agent has wide leeway for using his own judgment. He tries to base his judgment on perceptible fact as much as possible, but the personality of the taxpayer is bound to influence him too, even though he may not realize it and may never admit it.

In the case of the fellow who denied me the simple kindness of a cup of coffee, I was considerably tougher than usual on his travel and entertainment deductions. Normally I ask a TP to substantiate maybe half a dozen items picked at random, and if he scores tolerably well I let him go. In this case I made the man substantiate about 20 items, caught him short and whacked him with a deficiency that made his jaw drop. I felt ashamed of myself later, but the trouble was really his fault, not mine.

This should be obvious to most sensible people. What is not so obvious is the opposite truth: that it is not a good idea to cuddle up too close to a revenue agent. In the first place, I don't want to become your friend while I am auditing you. I don't want to become too fond of you. I made that mistake a few times when I was young and new in the business, but I don't make it anymore, and neither does any veteran tax man.

I recall auditing a likable old gentleman who, after retiring from a city police force, had started a fixit shop where he repaired people's lawnmowers, electric toasters and other gadgets and also did a little retailing of small appliances. His wife was in the hospital, and he was barely paying his bills. He didn't complain, however, and I admired his good cheer. He showed me around his shop and gave me instructions on how to fix my wife's electric mixer. In the process I grew too fond of him.

Going over his tax accounts I discovered that he had made a mathematical error in adding up his income. He had slipped a digit and ended with a total that was $1,000 too low. It was an understandable error; except for his $6,000 police pension, his income was composed of hundreds of small cash payments from his customers.

I started to correct the error, then hesitated. The change would result in his being billed for some $300 more income tax. I didn't want to see it happen. He couldn't afford $300.

Cash incomes like his are essentially unverifiable. It is up to the auditing agent to decide, partly subjectively, whether the taxpayer has stated the income honestly. If the agent determines that everything looks all right, that is usually the end of the matter. So I let the error go by. I pretended not to have noticed it. When I left, the cheery old TP had a $20 refund coming from overpayment of his estimated tax.

I wasn't happy with what I had done. Not only had I violated the trust placed in me by the U.S. government, but also—a more practical problem—I had deliberately thrown away $300 that could have gone toward fulfillment of my production quota. A foolish and sentimental act. I swore never to let it happen again. Though I broke that promise on two or three other occasions, in time I learned.

Thus the agent who audits you, unless he is very young, will resist any attempt you might make to grow too friendly. What may be just as important is that your attempt, should you make it, will look silly to him and will irritate him and may even disgust him.

Let's face it: A taxpayer and an auditing agent are natural adversaries. You and I can behave like adults as we go through your tax return, and there is no reason why we need snarl at each other. Yet we *are* sitting at opposite sides of the table. Under the circumstances I won't believe you if you pretend to think I'm a wonderful fellow. I will know you are lying. Your playacting won't convince me. It will seem like bootlicking, and I won't like it.

I remember one taxpayer, a high-salaried executive in a chemicals company, who kept putting his arm around my shoulders as though we were old college buddies. "You know, I *like* you," he kept saying. "I like a man who does his job well. I wish I had you as my accountant instead of the shmoe I've got."

This only annoyed me. It annoyed me so much after a while that to fend the man off I deliberately turned prickly. I went out of my way to find trouble spots in his return, much farther than I would have gone if he had let me alone. I gave him trouble over a trust fund he had set up for his kids, and over certain financial arrangements he had made with his divorced wife, and over a number of other things. The worst trouble of all arose over some automobile-mileage deductions.

He claimed to have driven some 15,000 miles on com-

pany business in his own car, without direct reimburse-
ment. I was so annoyed with him that I did something I
almost never do: I made him prove he owned the car in
the first place. This was sheer grumpiness on my part.
Revenue agents almost always assume a taxpayer owns a
car if he says he does, for our time is limited and there are
things on which we simply have to take the TP's word.
But in this case I wanted to create a nuisance and get the
taxpayer's arm off my shoulders.

It turned out that he owned no car at all. He didn't
even have a driver's license.

I handed the case to the intelligence division. A special agent discovered that the nondriver had been claiming car costs as tax deductions for years back. He was
finally socked with a heavy tax deficiency, plus interest,
plus a civil-fraud penalty. None of this would have happened if he had skipped the silly business of trying to be
my buddy.

Women taxpayers can be equally bad offenders in this
respect, if not worse. I am perfectly happy if a woman
offers me some coffee, or moves a lamp so as to improve
the light where I'm working, or performs any other act of
ordinary kindness and courtesy. But there is a point at
which too many such acts, repeated too often, become dis-
tracting and annoying. I enjoy having my wife and daugh-
ters fuss over me on rare occasions such as Father's Day
(in fact, to be truthful, I wallow in it), but in the adversary situation of a tax audit such fussing is less pleasant to
an agent. It is an overobvious attempt to curry favor.

The only taxpayer I ever shouted at was a woman.
She was an interior designer with an excellent income and
a very complicated tax return. She wouldn't let me do my
work. She kept asking if I was comfortable. "Why don't

you sit in this chair instead? Let me give you a cushion for your back. . . ." She served coffee with little cakes and tried to make me eat all of them. "Try one of these pink ones. . . ." She was driving me crazy. The end came when I was struggling with a long computation in which I had to juggle several variables in my head at once.

"Maybe you'd like to take your jacket off?" she said.

I yelled, "For God's sake, quit fluttering around!"

She sat down, shocked. I apologized immediately, of course. IRS inspectors are not pleased with agents who lose their cool during audits. But my loss of control had its effect. The lady TP sat quietly from then on and came through the audit with only a minor bill for additional tax. We parted amicably.

Some women go father than that. Occasionally an agent will hear a suggestion—usually, but not always, subtle—of companionship and sexual solace. But that comes under the heading of bribery and is a subject by itself. What is much more common is the superficially sexy kind of approach in which a woman TP tries to soften the agent by appealing to his male ego. I've had lady taxpayers tell me I'm handsome, for example. I have lived enough years to be certain that the face in my shaving mirror is distinctly not handsome. This kind of approach only irritates the average agent. It even irritates the breed of agent who would succumb to direct sexual bribery. "If the lady really wants to go to bed with me I'll listen," a special agent once told me in a fit of confession. "But it makes me mad if she only wants to tease me."

IRS has recently been hiring women agents in increasing numbers, and they appear to have the same trouble with male taxpayers. Worse, perhaps. "If they don't quit, I'll quit," a woman auditor told me morosely.

"The next time a taxpayer tells me he didn't know they made revenue men so pretty, I'll—I'll—"

"Audit the hell out of him," I suggested.

2. The Soothing Quality of Speed

It is true of any adversary situation, including a tax audit, that you can usually advance your own position by first asking yourself what your opponent wants. The tax man across the table from you has some motives opposed to your own, but he also wants at least one thing you want: *a quick audit.* If you work with instead of against him in achieving this goal, you may find him considerably more willing to go along with you in other respects.

Let's examine the agent's motives briefly. One thing he patently wants is tax money. His superiors at his local or district office judge him partly by his "production" of additional taxes. Some offices and group chiefs are more demanding in this respect than others, but it is altogether likely the agent is working toward a felt, if not explicitly stated, quota: He must bring in money to justify his job. This motive of his is directly opposed to your motive: What you want, naturally, is to get out of the audit with no additional taxes recommended.

But the agent also works under another quota that is more in line with your own wishes. He is not only required to produce in terms of tax money, but also in terms of the number of cases he closes. At many offices, case-closing is emphasized over money production. The faster the agent can get through his audits, the more cases he can close; and the more he closes, the more likely he is to win raises and promotions.

He will be especially anxious to finish with you rapidly if, after his first quick scanning of your accounts, he guesses there is little or no extra juice to be squeezed out of you. There is no sense wasting a lot of time on a dry orange. If your return looks basically correct and the agent figures you for zero deficiency or a paltry 50 bucks, he will want to get out fast and find juicier fruit.

You will want to speed him on his way for a number of reasons. From the TP's point of view, long audits are a damned nuisance at best, painful at worst. They waste your time, keep you from your job or from whatever else you would rather be doing. Moreover—and this is probably the most important reason of all—the longer an audit lasts, the greater are the odds that the examining agent will find problems that will cost you money.

A pleasant kind of momentum develops toward the end of a smooth, fast audit. The agent goes down his checklist item by item, finishing each task a little faster than the one before. As the end draws near he begins to look at his watch with eager anticipation. He thinks, "Hot dog, I'll be finished by four!" He mentally contemplates the gorgeous cold beer he is going to buy himself. He grows so happy that he is unwilling to let anything interfere with his little program. If he stumbles across a potential problem while in this euphoric state, he will be strongly tempted to pretend he didn't notice it.

So it is excellent strategy on your part to make the job go smoothly and fast. Your return ought to be neat, preferably typed. Agents hate returns on which they can't read the figures quickly. Also, be sure all your documentation is stacked and bundled in good order so you can find anything the agent asks for without a lot of scrabbling around. Your canceled checks should be in numerical order, not jumbled in an old shoebox. Few things make agents madder than the kind of taxpayer who can't find anything. "I *know* it's here someplace," the TP says, burrowing in old envelopes to find a canceled check. The agent sits and watches gloomily, wondering what his wife will say when he's late for dinner again. After waiting for a reasonable time the agent gets fidgety. He says, "Well, if you can't find it, I'm afraid we'll have to—." "No, no!" says the TP. "It's *got* to be here somewhere! I saw it just the other day!" He picks up an old accordion file and looks inside hopelessly. The bottom drops out, and a million crumpled sales slips, insurance policies, snapshots, letters and Christmas cards, along with an old cigarette lighter and some souvenirs of the TP's trip to the Grand Canyon, cascade onto the untidy heaps of paper that already litter the table. The agent contemplates the cold dinner ahead and thinks, *Oh, Lord. . . .*

What often happens in a situation like this is that the agent seeks other ways to occupy his time. While the taxpayer is hunting futilely for documentation of the mortgage interest he claims to have paid, the agent pokes through other papers and idly performs calculations that he might otherwise have skipped. He is in a grumpy mood by now. He may even suspect the taxpayer's failure to find things can be explained by the fact that the things don't exist. In this state of irritable idleness the agent may pounce on problems that would have slipped past him under happier circumstances.

I once audited a magnificently untidy man who ran an artesian-well company. It was a little one-truck outfit. His office was in his home. He earned his income by drilling and repairing wells, mainly for homeowners, but occasionally for builders or real-estate developers. This kind of income is tough to verify, for there is no convenient way in which a revenue agent can cross-check it against other records. If a fellow drills a well for your home and you pay him a thousand bucks, he can hide that income and have an excellent chance of getting away with it. You aren't likely to report the payment to IRS, for it isn't a tax deduction for you. The thousand becomes part of the capital cost of your home. It will show up in your tax records only when you sell the home, probably years after the well was drilled.

Faced with unverifiable income like this, an agent relies on various kinds of secondary evidence. I asked the well driller to show me his company's books, his bank records and sundry other documents. He handed me untidy sheafs of crumpled, dog-eared paper: an appalling mess. I combed through the sheafs with him and, after hours of work, found just enough internal consistency to convince me he probably wasn't cheating on a major scale. A few points troubled me a little. It seemed to me, for instance, that he was paying out more in wages than was consistent with his company's stated volume of business. But he argued that he had a bad back, couldn't do much of the manual work himself and so was forced to hire extra crewmen. In the end I took his word for it because I didn't know that much about the well business.

When we came to his personal affairs we waded into another swamp of paper. He could barely find anything. One thing he couldn't find was an automobile sales contract, needed to substantiate a deduction for state sales tax. While he was hunting for it in a rusty file box I sat there morosely, wishing for a beer and idly flipping through a book of check stubs. As I did so I noticed something odd.

He kept a single checking account for both business and personal use. This isn't uncommon with small businesses. What struck me as odd was that so many of the checks represented tax deductions. There were very few of the nondeductible checks that the average family man writes every month: checks to department stores, insurance companies, the milkman and so on. There weren't even many checks made out to cash.

I wondered: Could he have a second checking account at another bank? An account into which he dumped income that he didn't want me to find?

These mean thoughts would never have come to me if the taxpayer had made the audit go faster. But now, as he scrabbled through his snowdrifts of paper in search of the elusive car contract, I examined his checking records more closely. I noted that over a three-month period he had paid no money from that account to any dairy company, any department or apparel store, any life-insurance company. His tax return said he had four dependent children. Can you run a family of that size without buying milk or clothes? Maybe the family didn't like milk. Maybe the man's wife bought all the family's clothes for cash. And yet . . .

I stood up and told the taxpayer I was going to give him more time to find the car contract and the dozen other documents he had mislaid. "I'll phone you and set up another appointment in a week or so," I said.

On my way out I looked for a milkbox by the door. There it sat, with the diary company's name printed on it.

Back at my office I phoned the dairy's accounting department and asked how the taxpayer paid his milk bills. The bookkeeper said she thought he probably paid like nearly everybody else, by mailing in checks. I asked if she remembered the bank on which his checks were drawn. She said no, but the current month's bills were due to be paid in the next couple of weeks, and if I liked she would get the name for me when his check came in. I said I would like that very much.

It was as I suspected. When the bookkeeper phoned me with the bank's name a week later, it was not the bank where the well driller kept his declared account. He had been double-banking and double-booking me.

I turned the matter over to intelligence. Special agents went to the TP's second bank, probed back through several years of records and were able to establish something like $45,000 of undeclared income.

That $45,000 could have stayed hidden, cozily sheltered from taxation, if the well driller had had his papers in better order. During the subsequent investigation he asked me how I had stumbled onto his game, and when I told him, he grinned sadly and nodded. "I always meant to get myself organized," he said. "I guess the moral is if you're going to cheat, cheat neatly."

I am not sure whether that is actually a moral. But it is certainly a useful point to bear in mind.

3. The Sound of Honesty

One thing you should never, never do is tell a revenue agent how honest you are. There will be no reason for him to believe the statement. Worse, it will make him uncomfortable and may affront him. The statement carries within it a suggestion that the taxpayer, being a man of honor, does not expect other men of honor to doubt his word. It suggests that the agent will reveal himself as a petty and mean-minded fellow if he presumes to question figures on the taxpayer's return.

Some taxpayers actually do seem insulted when I question their returns. "Isn't my word good enough?" they ask angrily. I am obliged to tell them no, their word isn't good enough. The concept of honor is meaningful around a card table or on a schoolboys' playing field, but it has no place in the income-tax business. It only gets in the way.

More common than the insulted TP is the type who gives me a silly little character sketch of himself to demonstrate his unimpeachable honesty.

"I often think I'm the world's worst sucker," one fellow said, with a totally unconvincing chuckle. "I'm the kind of guy, if a store forgets to bill me for something, I'll remind them about it."

This kind of foolishness cuts no ice with me. Even though the character sketch may be accurate, I have no way of knowing it. As one of my instructors pointed out when I first joined the Revenue Service, the statement "I never lie" may itself be a lie and in fact usually is.

An examining agent must make some judgment about the taxpayer's honesty, but he doesn't do it by listening to what the TP says about himself. He does it by looking for clues, and sometimes by asking trick questions.

The most convincing clue, from my viewpoint, is the taxpayer's ability to document figures on his return. If you have submitted a list of 30 or 40 claimed payments to doctors, for example, I will pick three or four at random and ask to see canceled checks or other substantiation. If you can come up instantly with the checks, that will make me very happy. I will then assume you have been honest (that silly word again) about the rest of your doctor claims and I won't check them any further. When we move to other difficult parts of your return—your charity claims, for instance—I will be prepared to believe nearly everything you say and will do only a minor amount of spot-checking. As a matter of fact I may do none. If you have convinced me you're a careful collector of documents, and if I am anxious to go home, I'll go.

The taxpayer who arouses my suspicions is the one who, instead of documents, offers excuses. "Well, you just *happen* to have picked a doctor bill I paid in cash, and unfortunately I've lost the receipt. See, it happened this way. . . ." Two or three times during an audit, this is understandable and acceptable. But when it begins to become clear that the TP can hardly substantiate anything, we've got problems. This taxpayer will have to go through the mill. I've got to assume he is cheating. He is guilty until he proves otherwise.

I may ask him trick questions. There are limitless possibilities. A revenue agent, after being in the profession for a year or so, learns how to set all kinds of traps.

There is the External-Inconsistency Trap. Taxpayer has deducted state cigarette tax (this was allowable in the 1960s, though it isn't anymore). Agent offers him a cigarette. Taxpayer says, "No, thanks, I don't—uh, well, I have a sore throat today. Harrumph."

Or the Internal-Inconsistency Trap. Taxpayer shows a check to prove he paid $300 to a doctor for an eye operation. Agent asks, "Weren't you reimbursed by medical insurance?" Taxpayer says no. Agent says, "That's funny. You've taken deductions for Blue Shield. . . ."

Or the Calendar Trap, an Internal Inconsistency variant. Agent remarks conversationally that he is feeling overworked, plans to take a week's vacation this winter. "Yeah, I wish I could do that," TP says, stepping into the trap. "Trouble is I can't get away in winter. I always have to go in August." Agent says, "How long do you get?" TP says, "The whole month." Trap closes. Agent says, "That's odd. It says here you drove to Detroit on company business August fifteenth. . . ."

Or the Fumbled-Detail Trap. Agent says, "You give a lot of cash donations to your local church, I see." TP says, "Right, ten bucks every Sunday." Agent says, "That's a lot. You must like the church." TP says he does. Agent says, "It's the minister who makes a church, I think." TP agrees. Agent says, "What's your minister's name?" TP says, "His name? It's—uh—isn't that funny, I know it as well as my own—um, Smith. Right, that's it. Reverend Smith."

Traps such as these can convince an agent that he is dealing with a taxpayer whose statements must all be checked with care. Conversely, there are certain tricks the taxpayer can use to soothe the agent's suspicious nature.

The Conspicuous-Honesty Attack is probably the most common. It is useful against young agents—those under 30, let's say. Older agents have seen it too many times to be greatly impressed, but it may count with them sometimes and at worst it will amuse them. You say to the agent, "Listen, there's something I ought to tell you before we start. I made a mistake here in my charity deductions. That donation to the Wildlife Federation was only five bucks, not fifty. I slipped a zero in there somehow when I was doing my return, and I only just noticed it when I was going over my records for the audit. . . ."

The agent, if he is old enough and cynical enough, will suspect you made the mistake deliberately for purposes of mounting this attack. Fear not, however. The worst that can come of it is a minor tax deficiency. The best is that you will seem to grow a faint halo in the agent's eyes.

Then there is the At-Your-Mercy Approach. You tell

the agent, "Look, there are some deductions here that I can't substantiate. I know it was probably dumb of me, but I took the deductions anyway. I didn't know how else to handle the problem. So I'll leave it up to you. If you want to disallow them, well, what can I say? I have no way to defend them. . . ."

The agent may guess at the real reason why you can't substantiate the deductions: They are fake. But you have put yourself in a good strategic position. The agent may allow the deductions, or at least some of them, which will be dandy. Even if he disallows most or all of them, however, you have preserved your halo. You are far better off than if the agent had discovered the problem on his own and put you in the position of defending the indefensible.

4. Please, No Politics

A serious tactical error being made by increasing numbers of taxpayers these days, particularly younger taxpayers, is to gripe about the ways in which the tax money will be spent. Such griping is proper in various public forums and ultimately in the voting booth, but it is out of place in a tax audit.

I have sworn several times (though I have never followed words with action—not so far) that I would go out of my way to invent problems for the next taxpayer who groused to me about the Vietnam War. It is not fair to make me the scapegoat.

"What's all this money for, to buy more bombs?" one young woman demanded of me in a shrill voice. "It's blood-stained money. Aren't you ashamed to be collecting it?"

I kept my mouth shut. Agents are specifically warned against getting into political discussions during audits, and even without the warning most of us would avoid politics in any case. Like any citizen I hold my own political views, which I express at the right times. But during an audit I am apolitical. My job is simply to collect money for the government. The government will continue to need $200 billion a year no matter what political faction gets into power.

"What am I paying you for?" an older man said. "To send a couple more damned fools to the moon?"

"I wouldn't mind paying if I knew there was honesty in government," grumbled a department-store executive. "But my money will just get eaten up in graft and corruption. It goes from me to you to some politician's pocket. Why should I stand for it?"

Leave the poor agent alone. You will only make him mad. As you should know by now, it is not a good idea to make an enemy out of a revenue agent.

5. Bargaining Without Actually Bargaining

If you look an office auditor or revenue agent in the eye and ask him whether he will make a bargain with you, he will probably reply, "No, I can't make deals with taxpayers."

But the fact is that in all likelihood he will be quite amenable to a bargain if you approach him in the right way. In a typical bargain the agent agrees to allow or ignore *this* if the taxpayer agrees not to make a fuss over *that*. But the bargain is seldom explicitly stated as such. The agent and the taxpayer both understand clearly that a bargain has been struck, but they don't say so.

Each of you brings certain elements of strength to the bargaining table. The agent's strengths are obvious; he has the whole U.S. government behind him, and that is a lot of government. In your case, bargaining power will derive from two key facts about the agent. You should never forget these facts. One: He wants a quick audit: Two: He wants to close the case.

You can frustrate both these objectives if you believe it will be to your advantage. If the agent makes a decision you think wrong, you are legally entitled to argue with him and a lot of other people for a long, long time. He doesn't want that to happen if he can avoid it. Thus you start your move toward a bargain by making sure *he* knows *you* know how long you can keep the case open.

If you and the agent can't agree on some disputed item, your first step of appeal takes you in for a so-called district conference. This is essentially little more than an informal chat with a fellow from the district office having jurisdiction over you and the agent. District conferees are supposed to be (and surprisingly often are) fair to taxpayers.

If the dispute isn't settled there, you next go to an appellate conference. This is simply another step upward in the chain of command at IRS. An appellate conference is generally informal. Your chances of a fair hearing are good. You can bring a lawyer if you like, but probably won't need one unless you are arguing about a substantial sum of money. There may be more than one appellate conference, the second one somewhat more formal and lawyerish than the first.

If you get nowhere at the appellate level, you step out of IRS and go to the U.S. Tax Court, run by the Justice Department. If the argument involves less than $1,000 you go to an informal small-cases tax court where you can argue your case without a lawyer if you like. The tax courts are run by circuit-riding judges who go where the taxpayers are. In the small-cases court you and an IRS man will argue either before a judge or before a referee, who maybe a moonlighting young lawyer from your locality.

If the tax court leaves you dissatisfied, you next go to the U.S. Circuit Court of Appeals. However, you are now getting into sparsely populated territory. Only a tiny fraction of tax cases get this far, and if you try to scare a revenue agent by threatening to carry your hundred-dollar case beyond the tax court, he will know you are kidding. If you go still farther and start gibbering about the Supreme Court, he will guffaw.

It's the levels of appeal up to and including the tax court that are open to you in a practical sense, and this will be a source of your bargaining strength. Naturally, you would rather not get involved in appeals if you can help it. Appeals are time-consuming and, worse, expensive for the middle-income TP who must take time off from work to argue his case. Thus it can be said, as a general rule, that you want the case closed just as earnestly as does the agent.

Therefore, you bargain. But you don't do it in a direct or explicit way. It generally goes something like this:

Agent: Sorry, commuting expense isn't deductible. I've got to disallow it.

TP: But it's deductible if a man has to haul heavy equipment back and forth in his car.

Agent: Sometimes, but in your case that doesn't apply. You'd drive your car to work anyway. How else would you get there?

TP: I'd join a car pool.

Agent: I can't buy it.

TP (subtly showing he knows his rights): Well, I guess I'll have to tell it to a district conferee.

Agent: That's your privilege.

TP (starting to show the corner of a bargaining card): I've got to hold my ground on this one. Jeez, you've been hitting me right and left. That deduction for night-school costs, for instance. I'm sure it's valid, but you disallowed that one too.

Agent (feinting as he prepares to give ground): Well, hell, I told you my reasons. You can only deduct education costs if they improve your skills in your present job. Looks to me like you're in school to learn a whole new field.

TP: Not so. I can even show you a place in a company manual where it says raises and promotions depend on this kind of education. We're supposed to broaden ourselves. I'm in competition with other guys who have this schooling. How else can I compete?

Agent: Well, I don't know. We're into some fuzzy areas where there are no hard answers. I don't say I'm infallible, but I've got to make these judgments. . . .

TP: Listen, will it make you happy if I show you that company manual? You'll see it in black and white, all about education and career advancement.

Agent: Well, I don't know. . . .

The agent actually knows very well. He will pretend reluctance for a while longer, and finally the unstated bargain will be sealed.

6. Cheatsmanship

If you feel compelled to seek economic survival by cheating (for advice on which see Chapter 14), remember one thing and remember it well: Don't ever admit to an auditor or agent that you have cheated deliberately.

The agent will guess you have cheated on purpose—

indeed, may know it for sure. He is not a fool. When he catches you with a faked deduction or a batch of undeclared income, the facts will probably speak for themselves. But whatever happens, don't make it worse by blurting out a confession. Don't say, "I should have known I couldn't get away with it," or anything of the kind. Instead, mumble excuses. Any goofy excuses will do. "Gee, how could I have forgotten that?" Or, "My goodness, how did it happen?" Or, "I didn't know I was supposed to declare that." Or, if you prefer, say nothing.

There are at least two excellent reasons for this. The first is that if you are headed for a fraud investigation you should be aware that anything you say may be used against you. The agent is supposed to warn you about this at the moment he decides to turn the case over to intelligence, but he may neglect to do so. You should also be aware that to prove fraud the government must prove you cheated deliberately. The deliberateness is what counts—the state of mind—not the mere fact that you have underpaid your tax. By admitting that you cheated on purpose you may hang yourself before the trial even starts. Thus your most prudent course is simply to mumble. If a fraud case actually develops, say nothing further until you have seen a lawyer.

The second good reason for watching your words is that in all likelihood the agent would prefer not to make a fraud case out of it. He knows fraud is difficult to prove. His group chief would rather have him out in the field producing than cooling his heels in a courtroom. He scores no points by nailing a lot of taxpayers for fraud.

Unless your transgression is so flagrant that it can't conceivably be ascribed to anything but willful cheating, the agent will lean far to find another explanation. He will want to go along with your mumbled excuse. All he really seeks is your tax money, not your hide. You will make life complicated for him if you stand there like a penitent and confess willful intent to defraud the government.

In this respect, at least, he is on your side. His fond wish is to go away, bearing your signature on a simple deficiency agreement, and never see you again.

Chapter 14

THE MIDDLE-INCOME TAXPAYER'S CHEATING GUIDE

The U.S. income-tax law is based on some pious and grand-sounding theories that don't work. To be charitable, perhaps I should say nobody has yet found a way to make them work. That implies hope for the future and is comforting as well as charitable. But that particular future is a place we may not get to right away. If you are interested in saving tax dollars this year instead of in some utopian future year—and I'm *very* interested in doing that myself—you have no choice but to deal with the messed-up situation that exists in the present.

We've admired the basic theory of the graduated income tax—that everybody pays according to his ability to pay. That sounds lovely. As we have noted, however, the heaviest burden sits like a million tons on the bent back of the poor old middle class. The high rates supposedly paid by the rich are hardly more than a fiction authored by Congress to keep the middle masses happy. For Congress, having ordained the high rates at the top, has passed several thousand pages of alleviatory laws to make sure that hardly anybody actually pays those high rates. There are so many loopholes for the rich that the entire top half of the graduation can be called solid loop-hole. Air, in other words.

The AFL-CIO, among many groups examining this odd state of affairs, found in one study that the graduation of effective tax rates—that is, taxes actually paid—goes down-ward as you climb the income levels above the upper-middle class. The study showed that the average taxpayer with an income of $50,000 to $100,000 paid only 30.9% in the year covered, while the average TP earning more than $1 million a year paid still less: 28.7%. Even these rates may be overstated, for, you will recall, there are types of income enjoyed by the rich—interest on certain bonds, for example—that not only are tax-free, but needn't even be reported.

No effective legal dodges are easily available to the middle-income man or woman. If you are caught in the middle, dear old friend and TP, you have only two choices: You can pay a higher tax rate than the million-a-year man pays. Or you can cheat.

Nearly all American taxpayers cheat, at least to a minor extent. I don't like the idea of cheating, and in fact it is my job to catch cheats. At the same time, I am com-pelled to recognize that the system of taxation by confes-sions encourages cheating, and until a fairer and more sensible revenue-raising idea is invented, I cannot find it in my heart to blame a middle-income taxpayer whose desperate struggle for survival leads him to break the rules. I can sock him with a bill for what he failed to pay, but I can't blame him.

If you decide your survival depends on cheating, you should know the odds against you. You should also know that the punishment may be severe if you are caught. You'll be billed for back taxes plus 6% annual interest and possibly a 50% fraud penalty, and if your transgression is bad enough you may even end in jail. It is rare that a tax case becomes a criminal case with jail as the punishment, but the possibility should be kept in mind.

What follows is a listing of the more common cheating gambits used by middle-income taxpayers, the likelihood of being caught in each case, and the common mistakes and circumstances that lead to that unhappy outcome.

The Ghost Gambit

There are probably at least half a million working adults in this country who, although they earn incomes high enough to be taxable, have never filed tax returns and don't intend ever to file tax returns. Their income is made up entirely of small cash payments, and nobody ever files a W-2 withholding form or a 1099 information return on them, so IRS never learns of their existence. Among these ghostly folk are doctors in rural areas, general handymen, small storekeepers, domestic workers, self-employed craftsmen, prostitutes, gamblers and gypsy-taxicab owners. IRS will never catch most of these people. They can be tripped up only by an unlikely stroke of bad luck. Somebody may squeal on them, or a revenue agent might just happen to hear something that will arouse his curiosity and give rise to an investigation.

Once you file your first tax return, it becomes difficult

and risky to vanish ever again into that happy company of ghosts. It can be done, but it requires both clever planning and a spoonful of luck. Once you file, your name and Social Security number go into a computer memory bank at your IRS regional office. The little bit of data remains there, its tiny heartbeat throbbing quietly but steadily, until IRS becomes satisfied that you are dead. Death is the only foolproof escape.

If a year comes when you fail to file a return, the regional computer will notice your absence and will be saddened by it. Your name will be printed out with a long sorrowful list of other TPs who have failed to put in an appearance at that regional center that year. Routine checks will be made through the National Identity File in Washington, and most taxpayers on the list will be found simply to have moved from one region of the country to another. They will be found to have filed on schedule at other regional offices.

Those who seem not to have filed at all will be checked further. Many will turn out to be dead. Others will explain that they didn't earn enough money during the year to make a tax return mandatory. A few will offer excuses: They were sick in hospitals at tax time, for example. The remainder—a very small percentage—will appear to have vanished without a trace.

These phantom taxpayers will of course be hunted. But the hunt is not likely to be very grim or determined. In all likelihood what will happen is that a revenue officer or agent will be handed a short list of vanished taxpayers and asked to track them down. He may not get this list until the taxpayers have been missing for several years, for IRS is a huge organization, and its machinery turns with ponderous slowness. The agent may write a few letters and make a few phone calls, but if these produce no results he will probably file the list in his bottom desk drawer and hope nobody remembers giving it to him. He has tax-money and case-closing quotas to fulfill. Instead of hunting ghosts he would rather spend his time dealing with patently existent TPs whose bank accounts can be squeezed for instant juice.

If you want to escape the income tax by this route, obviously you must quietly subside into some occupation where people pay you in small cash and file no W-2s or 1099s saying what they paid and to whom. Obviously, too, you must move from where you now live, leaving neither a forwarding address nor any other readily discoverable clues to your new whereabouts. This is by no means easy to do, for in essence it means totally abandoning your old life, cutting all ties except perhaps those with a few close friends who can be trusted to keep their mouths shut.

It isn't easy, but the fact is that disgusted taxpayers try it every year. And some—how many, nobody knows—get away with it, permanently.

The Phantom-Kid Game

If you say you have six kids and hence are entitled to six personal exemptions for them, the odd fact is that IRS will probably believe you.

I'm not quite sure why this is so. I know only that tax-payers' exemption claims for kids are very rarely questioned. In all my time as a revenue agent, I've questioned such claims perhaps a dozen times in all. A dozen, out of thousands of audits. Never, unless my suspicions were aroused by some obvious inconsistency, have I asked a tax-payer to submit birth certificates or other proof that his claimed youngsters actually existed. Nor do I know any other agent who routinely asks for such proof. We demand proof of nearly everything else, but not kids. Kids simply are not part of the audit routine.

In every case where I've caught a taxpayer cheating this way, the clue was that something in either his return or his life-style, or both, was quite obviously out of synch with his claimed number of children. If he had thought about it a little while he would have spotted the inconsistency himself and abandoned the gambit before I came around.

You remember the case where I caught a fellow because his house looked too small to contain his claimed six kids, and there were no bikes or teddy bears or other childhood paraphernalia around the house.

In another case I became suspicious because a taxpayer's medical expenses looked abnormally low for the five-child family described on his tax return. Thinking that perhaps he had just had an unusually lucky year in terms of doctor bills, I checked some of his previous years' returns. His medical expenses had been unbelievably low every year. When I followed up my suspicions I found he was not only childless but a widower; his wife had died years before. He had continued to enter her on his return. He had forged her signature, thus getting the benefits of joint filing as well as six exemptions for people who didn't exist.

Another husband and wife tripped themselves by entering two phantom kids on their tax returns for too long a time—33 years, to be exact. I forget exactly how this bit of foolishness came to light. Somebody at regional headquarters had been probing through this couple's past history, and when I was sent out to audit them I was instructed to find out about their dependents. It turned out that a son and daughter did exist, but the son was 33 and the daughter 32, and neither was living with the parents. The father explained to me that he couldn't afford to lose the two exemptions when the kids matured, so he had simply gone on claiming them.

That happened in the mid-1960s. Today, IRS computers are programmed to question apparent inconsistencies of that kind. Obviously, if you must lie, you should at least lie convincingly.

The T&E Rip-offs

It is part of American tax lore that nearly everybody who claims travel and entertainment expenses resorts to at least some fiction. Revenue agents realize this fictionalizing goes on, but as long as you don't insult our intelligence by doing it too crudely, our inclination is to play along with you. We appreciate skillful fiction.

A taxpayer isn't required to come up with solid, documentary proof of every claimed T&E expense. The rules say you're supposed to have proof of hotel bills and other claimed items over $25, and I generally spot-check a few such items in the course of an audit. I ask the TP to show me a couple of hotel bills, credit-card vouchers or other documentation to support his claims. If he scores two out of three, and if my general feeling about him is that he's no worse a liar than the average, I let him go. Or I may suggest a small adjustment to justify my job—and he accepts the adjustment with relief.

In general I'm forced to take his word for almost all his T&E claims. This is partly because it would use up too much of my time to check them all, and partly because some of them are essentially unprovable in any case. If you say you drove from Cleveland to Chicago in your car, how can I argue with you?

But the fiction must be well wrought. Most taxpayers write down their T&E fiction in diaries or ledger books, and many of them perform this creative work the night before the audit. If you must do this, make sure the result is believable. Don't make it too neat. A record honestly kept over a year's time is seldom neat. The penmanship tends to vary; some entries may be in ink while others are in pencil; and so on. Furthermore, the record book itself becomes scruffy and dog-eared.

As a critic of T&E fiction, I give bad reviews to neat work. I recall one taxpayer who handed me a pocket diary so new that it creaked when I opened it. I knew damned well that he had composed all the entries the day or week before. So instead of being content with the usual quick spot-check, I demanded proof of dozens of items, caught him short and ended by disallowing more than half his T&E total. His book of fiction, in other words, did not sell.

Another T&E novelist tripped himself by going too far in the opposite direction. The ledger book he handed me was dramatically scuffed and bent, he had dripped tea or coffee with great care on some of the pages and he had even made a gorgeous cup ring on the front cover. I was prepared to give him a rave review. But then I noticed a peculiar symmetry in the entries. He had alternated with perfect regularity: pencil, blue ink, green ink, all the way through the book. My suspicions aroused, I put him through the mill and ended by socking him with a fair-sized deficiency.

The Capital-Gain Dodges

This nation's economic system, including its tax law, is set up in such a way that the average middle-income man gets but little chance to accumulate wealth. Once in a while, however, he finds himself in possession of some piece of property—a house, a few shares of stock—that he can sell at a profit. The profit, if it fulfills certain requirements, is a capital gain. The choice he then faces is whether to declare the gain and pay the tax, or cheat and not declare it.

In the case of a house you are foolhardy to try to dodge the tax. There is no good way to hide the fact that you owned a house last year but don't own it this year. The agent looking over your return will spot the facts quickly. He may note that your address has changed. Even if you sold a summer cottage without changing your primary address, the agent will see other clues: Last year you paid a real-estate tax and claimed it as a deduction; this year you didn't. Last year you claimed mortgage interest as a deduction; this year you didn't. You may be able to offer acceptable explanations for these year-to-year changes, and you may be able to explain why you haven't declared a gain (maybe you sold at a loss; maybe you bought another house so as to defer the tax), but the agent's first thought will be, "Oh ho, this bears looking into!"

If you take the standard deduction rather than itemizing, your chances of hiding a house-sale gain are somewhat better. However, most people who own mortgaged real estate do itemize, for the mortgage interest and real-estate taxes generally push a taxpayer into an area where the standard deduction doesn't pay off.

As for the stock market, it would probably be quite safe to say that every weekday Wall Streeters make at least a million dollars in capital gains that my colleagues and I will never find out about. The total of undeclared stock gains could be higher than a billion dollars a year, for all I know. I do know that the total is enormous. For the fact is that IRS has never found an effective way to keep track of all those millions of transactions.

If you sell a stock on which you have been receiving dividends of more than $10 per year, then we've got you. You have been required to declare those dividends as income, and the company paying the dividends has been required to tell us the key facts about you every year. An agent looking over your return will notice that suddenly one year you stopped receiving those dividends. He will know beyond much doubt that you sold the stock, and he will then look to see whether you declared the gain, if any.

But there are thousands of stocks that pay no dividends, particularly on the huge over-the-counter market where some of the biggest capital-gain killings are made. When you sell a zero-dividend stock, there is no direct way in which IRS can discover the fact. Your broker isn't required to send us an information form or any other kind of tip-off.

Revenue officials have often plaintively asked the Wall Street brokerage community to be more cooperative, to adopt some kind of reporting form that would be sent to IRS every time somebody sells a stock. But the brokers have always howled with anguish and horror whenever this kind of talk came up and have lobbied grimly against the idea in Washington. Wall Street is already up to the ears in paperwork. To generate a new piece of paper for every stock transaction—of which there are millions a day —could swamp the Street.

Taxpayers who fail to declare stock gains can be caught in various ways, of course. Anytime I like, I can walk into a brokerage office and ask to see a TP's account records. The records will tell me what he has bought and sold over the years and at what prices, and if he has been cheating I've got him by the tail. But the chances that this will happen to any given market player are slight. There is no established routine for uncovering hidden stock gains on a mass basis. People who are caught cheating this way are caught individually and randomly.

The Capital-Loss Dodges

The rules say you can subtract certain realized losses from taxable gains in a given year, and if you come out with a net loss you can use it to reduce your taxes in that and future years, within certain restrictions. The object of the game is to show as large a bundle of realized losses as possible. This is one of the more popular sports on Wall Street.

"Realized"—that is the key word. If you've got some old hound dog of a stock that has lost half its value since the day you bought it, you aren't considered to have a loss for tax purposes unless you actually sell the stock (or unless, in rarer cases, it is officially declared worthless). Your loss may have occurred slowly over a number of years, but you generally get no tax break out of it until the year you finally sell.

Suppose you don't really want to sell? You figure maybe your old dog will wake up any month and go bounding uphill. Is there a way you can establish a tax loss yet still keep the stock? There is. It's called a wash sale. It is strictly against the rules, but thousands of stock players use the method every year, most often in December. My guess is that at least three-fourths of them get away with it.

To conduct a wash sale you sell the stock, and then you buy it back the same day or week. According to the Treasury's rules, the transaction is a wash sale—and hence is deemed not to establish any valid tax loss—if you buy back the stock (or a related security such as a warrant or call option on that same stock) within 30 days of selling it. Thus, the difficult part of the game—the challenge—is that of hiding the fact that you did buy back before 30 days were up.

You can, if you wish, simply trust this part of the venture to luck. The revenue agent who audits your return may be lazy or bored. Maybe he will have a hot date that evening and want to finish the audit fast and go home. In this case you will have no problem. You merely show him your broker's confirmation slips indicating the price at which you first bought your stock and the lower price at which you sold it, along with the dates and other relevant data. The agent may accept this documentation without demanding more, and you are home free.

But you may not be that lucky. Perhaps you have rubbed the agent the wrong way personally. Perhaps he simply doesn't like people with noses of your particular shape, hair of your length or socks of the color you happen to have picked that day. Perhaps his boss has recently given him a lecture about wash sales. Perhaps he is hung over and feeling grumpy. For these or a hundred other reasons, the agent may ask you to show him some of your broker's monthly account statements. If you can't (or claim you can't) find them, he can get the records from your broker easily enough. A quick examination of the records will show him that a wash sale has taken place.

How to avoid this unhappy outcome? The most popular gambit is to have two brokers. In conducting your wash sale, you sell your stock through Broker *A*, then buy it back through Broker *B*. When the revenue agent comes around, you take great care not to let him know about

Broker *B*. You show him confirmation slips and account statements and anything else he wants to see from Broker *A*. He probably will trouble you no further. He may suspect you keep a second broker around (we always suspect this when a TP has a lot of stock losses, especially when all or most are realized in December), but proving his suspicions would involve him in an enormous amount of work, more than your possible tax deficiency may be worth.

The Rental Razzle-Dazzle

An enormous amount of untaxed rental income flows into American citizens' pockets every year. It is supposed to be taxed, but IRS can't find it.

Among middle-income folks the most common situation of this kind arises when a taxpayer buys himself a second home: a summer cottage by a lake or sea, a ski lodge, a fishing cabin. Since he doesn't use it all 12 months of the year, he rents it to other families part of the time. If his second home is conveniently located near schools and is winterized, he may be lucky enough to keep it rented throughout the year except during his own vacation period. The income he gets from his tenants is just as taxable as his salary—if he reports it. If he elects not to report the rental income, his chances of getting away with the ploy are better than IRS likes to think about.

There is no established routine by which the Revenue Service can discover rental income of this kind. The tenant who pays the rent has no reason to say anything about it on his own tax return, for the rent is not tax-deductible to him. It would be wholly or partly deductible if he used the house for a business purpose, but if he uses it simply as a residence he gets no tax break out of it. Therefore, no report of the rent payments ever reaches us at IRS.

If you go into the landlord business and elect to hide rental income this way, you can be tripped by various random circumstances. The odds are in your favor, but you aren't totally safe. For example, it might happen by bad luck that your all-year tenant gets himself audited. A revenue agent, going over your tenant's tax return, may note the absence of deductions for mortgage interest and real-estate tax and he will deduce the TP has been living in a rented home. The agent may then, just for fun, ask your tenant how much rent he pays and to whom. If he has time on his hands the agent may eventually run a quick check of your returns to find out whether you've been declaring that rental income. This chain of events isn't likely, but it is possible.

Another possibility, somewhat less remote, is that you will be tripped by an audit of your real-estate broker. Technically, a broker is supposed to file an information return saying how much rental income you earned during the year. In practice, many brokers don't bother. But if you depend on a broker to find tenants for you, the broker takes a commission from your tenants' rent payments. This commission is taxable income to the broker. A revenue agent, auditing the broker, might ask to see a list of all the people from whom the broker earned commissions during the year. Hoping to stir up some action, the agent might take this list back to his office and check some or all of the people on it—including, perhaps, you—to see how many have failed to declare rental income and/or capital gains from house sales.

If you are lucky, the broker himself will have been cheating. He won't have declared his entire income. The list he gives the revenue agent will omit mention of a number of rental transactions which the broker feels are essentially untraceable by IRS. One of these omitted transactions may be yours.

The Instant-Doctor Play

Medical expenses that exceed 3% of your adjusted gross income are deductible. This gives rise to a lot of interesting games, the most common of which is that of inventing doctors who don't exist.

A taxpayer who itemizes his deductions is required to submit, along with his tax return, a list of the doctors, dentists, psychiatrists and other practitioners to whom he paid money during the year. The average list contains the names of a dozen or more practitioners, and some big-family heads send in lists of 20 or 30. If IRS were to check with all the doctors on all these lists to find out whether the claimed payments were actually made for the purposes stated, we would need a staff of about a million people. The job would have to be done by human eye and hand, for computers are not yet clever enough to read ordinary typed or handwritten lists; nor are they clever enough to pick up a phone and say, "Dr. Parker, this is IRS calling. Do you really exist?" Because the doctor-checking job would be overwhelmingly huge and confusing, IRS makes only the barest token of an attempt to do it.

What generally happens is that a revenue agent runs a quick spot-check. He looks down your list of claimed doctor payments. If he sees a payment that is larger than the others he may question you about it. He asks you to show him a canceled check as proof of payment and he asks what the nature of the illness was. He may then pick a couple more claimed payments at random and ask you for canceled checks covering those. As long as there is nothing unusual in your return or your manner to arouse his suspicions, he lets it go at that. There is really little more he can do. He might—just might—check with one or two of the practitioners later on, to find out whether your daughter really had her teeth straightened and the bill really was $1,200. But he would be likely to do this only if he had some compelling reason to suspect you of cheating. A revenue agent is a busy man, with production quotas to fulfill. He simply can't afford to risk his time on wild-doctor chases. The nature of the system forces him to concenrate on efforts that promise the biggest payoffs in terms of new tax money brought in.

Thus, suppose you have stated on your doctor list that you paid $200 to a Sigmund Schrunkenkopf, M.D., psychiatrist. The agent asks you for the canceled check. You show it to him. He examines it, nods and is satisfied.

The truth is that old Sig Schrunkenkopf never went near a medical college and can't even affix a Band-Aid without getting the two ends stuck together. He is, in fact, a plumber. The $200 you paid him was for work he did around your wife's laundry room. You made the check out to plain Sigmund Schrunkenkopf, holder of no medical degrees. When he cashed the check and it came back to you, canceled, you wrote "M.D." after his name.

Each April 15, thousands of instant doctors spring into existence by means such as that. The most common types of instant doctors are people who are legitimately doctors of something other than human medicine. Veterinarians, for example. Doctors of jurisprudence. Church ministers. If you make a check out to a "Dr. George Smith" in payment for goods or services of any kind, the canceled check will have a distinctly medical look when you hand it to a revenue agent. George Smith, indeed, may not hold a doctoral degree at all, in medicine or anything else. He may simply be a good friend of yours. He is well known at his bank, and the tellers there will accept checks on which his name is misspelled or on which he is occasionally styled "Dr." by mistake. In December you give him a check for a hundred bucks. He cashes the check and gives the cash back to you. You claim him as a medical expense, with the canceled check to prove it.

The Phantom-Burglar Ploy

If something is stolen from you during the tax year, the uninsured loss in excess of $100 is tax-deductible. Another game is afoot!

(That $100 floor is the result of some bureaucratic reasoning that doesn't seem very bright to me. I won't harp on it here, except to note that it seems unfair to the non-rich TP to whom $100 is a lot of money. A rich man or woman may own an uninsured thousand-dollar watch or bracelet and can get a tax break if it is stolen. A man in my middling salary bracket tends to own a $59.98 watch. If it is stolen the Treasury will weep no tears and offer no aid.)

If you choose to invent a theft that did not take place, it will be incumbent upon you to present the fiction convincingly to the revenue agent who audits your return. He will be fully and cynically aware of the possibility that you are lying. In fact he will probably suspect, as I do, that at least one out of every two thefts claimed on tax returns never actually took place. However, he will be at a disadvantage: He won't be able to ask for direct documentation. There can't be any; a thief never leaves a signed statement for the TP's convenience at tax time. The agent will have to rely mainly on indirect evidence. In the last analysis it will be his word against yours.

The agent will first ask you to demonstrate that you actually owned the thing you say was stolen, and he will next want some evidence of its value. This will require a little work. If you still have a sales slip to prove you once bought a $300 set of golf clubs, you are highly unusual. Hardly anyobdy saves sales slips in so organized a way that he can find a specific slip when he needs it, especially when it is several years old. As a matter of fact I grow very suspicious when a TP comes up with an old sales slip to prove ownership and value of something allegedly stolen. I suspect he just happened to find the slip one day while cleaning out his desk. Having found it and having noted that it indicated an amount of money greater than $100, he was suddenly hit by the grand idea of using it in a fake-theft ploy.

Lacking a sales slip or other handy documentation, you may have to go back to the store where you bought your golf clubs, or whatever you say was stolen, and ask for a written statement or a copy of the bill. Or go to the pro at your golf course and ask him to say, in writing, that he recalls seeing you with a set of Brand X clubs, whose market value he estimates at $275. A bottle of good Scotch will, of course, do wonders for his memory.

In the case of lost cash, obviously, there is no easy way to show ownership or prove value. If you claim to have been robbed of cash, the revenue agent will be more or less obliged to take your word as to the amount. But the amount must be reasonable—must be consistent with your income level and life-style. If you claim to have been carrying $2,000 in cash when you were mugged, you had better have an excellent explanation of why you were carrying so much.

I recall auditing one fellow who claimed to have lost a $1,000 bill to a pickpocket. Since this TP was in the $15,000-a-year bracket, I found his story most unlikely. Why would such a man be carrying a negotiable grand in his pocket? He explained that he had been carrying it as a gag. He had cashed in some savings bonds, he said, and for fun had asked the bank to give him part of the proceeds in the form of a $1,000 bill. That night he had gone to his favorite bar, ordered a glass of beer and offered the big bill in payment. "Sorry, this is the smallest I have," he had said. It was all part of some running gag that had been going on at that bar for years, he explained to me. According to his story the crowd at the bar was vastly amused.

I checked the story with both the bank and the bartender, and it was true. I finished the audit perfectly satisfied that the man had actually carried a $1,000 bill in his pocket. I wasn't at all satisfied that this bill had been stolen, however. I think the idea of faking the theft came to him as he gazed contemplatively into the suds of his third or fourth beer at the bar that night. But I had no evidence to support my suspicions, so I was forced to allow him a $900 deduction.

Demonstrating that the alleged theft took place—this is the easiest part of the venture for the taxpayer; the hardest part for the revenue agent. All the agent can do is ask you to show that you took the steps a citizen would normally take after being robbed. Did you go to the police? Did you check with your insurance company? If your wallet was stolen did you cancel your old credit cards and get a new driver's license?

It is as easy to lie to the police, obviously, as to a revenue agent. Police departments in many cities earn considerable revenue by selling documents bearing titles such as "Loss Verification Form." A taxpayer gets such a form simply by going to a police station and saying, "I been robbed!"

The cop at the desk says, "Okay, fill out this form." The form asks what was stolen and what its value was.

The cop says, "You want us to countersign it and give you a copy back? You know, for income tax?"

The taxpayer says, "Gee, that would be great!"

The cop says, "Ten bucks, please."

The taxpayer, though lighter by ten bucks, goes away with an official document that he will be able to show to a revenue agent. Neither the revenue agent nor the cop will necessarily believe a theft actually happened.

"It's amazing how many burglaries and muggings get reported to us around Christmastime," a cynical old police captain once told me. "I once read a thing by some psychologist. He was trying to show how Christmas gets people upset and makes them do crazy things. The Christmas Blues, he called it. Used some of our statistics to prove his point. Showed December was the peak month for grand larceny. Well, hell. If you want the truth, people are no crazier at Christmas than any other time of year. December is the peak month for tax gimmicks is all."

Wondrous are the ways of TPs, but you should be warned that the Revenue Service is nobody's fool. From Washington headquarters to the most remote field office, revenue men are fully aware of every cheating system ever invented. Indeed, we know of some possible cheating systems that haven't even been tried yet.

IRS is constantly setting new traps for cheats. No trap

will catch everybody, but every trap catches somebody. A taxpayer who cheats must know he is running risks. What makes his situation worse is that he can never know precisely how great the risks are.

And finally it must be noted that every cheating system is self-limiting. There can be no perfect, risk-free system. Anytime a system gets too close to perfection, the Revenue Service makes extra efforts and assigns extra personnel to close it down.

Chapter 15

IS THERE A BETTER TAX THAN THE INCOME TAX?

Karl Marx once suggested that a steeply graduated income tax could be used as a bloodless, nonrevolutionary way to redistribute wealth in a capitalist country. When the U.S. Constitution was amended in 1913 to pave the way for an income tax in this country, Marx's endorsement was cited amid great floods of tears as an excellent reason for forgetting the whole dumb idea. "This is the beginning of the death of capitalism!" raged an official of the Investment Bankers Association. And a French observer, Yves Guyot, remarked sadly that the new tax law heralded the start of socialism and the end of a great nation's greatness.

Nobody need have worried, however. Marx tended to think of situations in idealized terms, and things seldom worked out in real life as he imagined or proposed on paper. The fact is, as we've noted, that graduated income taxes never seem to work right. They never achieve the grand-sounding purpose of making the richest citizens pay the biggest share of the society's operating expenses. The heaviest burden always falls on the middle class.

Over the years, many profound thinkers have tried to devise other ways to raise a government's needed cash. Each thinker has started with the same optimistic notion: There *must* be a better way; there must be something other than income to tax; and if we must tax income, there must be a fairer and more efficient way to frame the laws and administer them. There must be a more effective collection system. There must be a more workable weapon against cheating.

Some taxpayers I've audited through the years have come up with novel suggestions. One fellow proposed a kind of work tax, similar to those that were common centuries ago. Each citizen, he said, on graduating from school or college, should put in a mandatory five years' work in some government-operated industry. The citizen would work with no pay except room and board. The government would collect the profits from the industry. If there were enough such industries and the profits were big enough, the government wouldn't need to raise any additional revenues through taxation.

Could it work? Well, no. Modern government is so expensive that as things now stand the average U.S. citizen spends a third of his adult life working to pay taxes. If these taxes were paid directly in the form of work, the mandatory slave-labor requirement would have to be something like twenty years, not five.

Another TP, a woman executive, suggested that a citizen go totally and blissfully untaxed during his lifetime, but that his entire estate automatically escheat to the government on his death. In other words there would no longer be any income taxation, but to make up for that, there would no longer be any possibility of personal inheritance. This idea seemed curiously attractive to me when I first heard it propounded (the lady was not only smart, but charming, too). Yet its glories faded when I thought my way down to its gritty details. The Universal 100% Inheritance Tax, as it might be called, would offer such enormous opportunities to cheat that it might be unworkable. Moreover, it would have to be riddled with loopholes to take care of various inequities. Suppose a man died while still supporting minor children? Suppose a man and his son built up a company together? What part of the company would be considered "estate" at the man's death?

Still another taxpayer proposed what might be called a Neighborhood Tax. It was similar in some respects to the wealth-clue taxes of ancient times, under which citizens were taxed according to the number of slaves or horses they visibly owned. The basic premise of the Neighborhood Tax is that income can be hidden, but that an excellent clue to income is the type of neighborhood in which a taxpayer lives. Therefore, all the neighborhoods in the country should be assessed and divided into 20 or 30 categories, graduating from "dirt poor" to "filthy rich." There could then be a fixed annual tax on each residence in each type of neighborhood.

I pointed out to the man proposing this idea that there were some difficulties in it. Some residences don't clearly belong to any neighborhood. Moreover, it would be necessary in many cases to draw arbitrary dividing lines. The tax status of people living right on the line where a "moderately-medium-poor" neighborhood was deemed to border a lower-taxed "somewhat poor" one would be vague. Also, the tax would be unfair to a man who, because his family was large, was forced to live in a bigger and costlier house than he might otherwise have chosen.

The taxpayer replied to my objections by pointing out that our present income tax, too, is unfair to many, difficult to administer and shot through with arbitrary dividing lines. He felt the Neighborhood Tax had two large advantages that made it worth considering: It would be simple; and it would offer little opportunity for cheating. Perhaps he was right.

Now let's look at some alternative revenue-raising proposals that have been considered seriously in the scholarly world of economists.

Gross-income tax: In most variations of this proposed approach, you would be taxed on some amount of money roughly comparable to what is now labeled "adjusted gross income" on your Form 1040. In essence this means all the money you took in during the year, less the actual cost of producing the income. In the most extreme variations of the proposal there would be no deductions at all except those directly related to income production: no personal exemptions; no deductions for charity, medical expense, interest, state or local taxes; no special preferences such as the low-capital-gains rate.

One major attraction of the gross-income tax is its apparent simplicity. Dan Throop Smith, a Harvard Business School professor, put it neatly when he pointed out that in our present system "each deduction is a basis for controversy and provides a temptation for manipulation." By allowing only a few possible deductions instead of the confusing array we deal with today, the gross-income tax (ideally) would be easier for each taxpayer to figure out, would require fewer revenue men such as me for its administration and would offer less leeway for cheating.

Another attraction of the gross-income tax is that its percentage rates would presumably be lower than those we're used to. Since a man's or company's adjusted gross income is bigger than the net taxable income we now deal with, the government could get the same amount of revenue by setting the rates at, say, 5% to 25%, instead of our present 20% to 70%. Ideally, there would then be less of what tax theorists call "disincentive," an economically unhealthy state of mind that evolves whenever a taxpayer moves into the high brackets. He figures there is no profit in trying to get more income, since most of it will be taxed away from him. Instead, he spends an ever greater share of his time and energy trying to avoid taxes on what income he already has. This state of mind obviously doesn't help the country's economy grow. But if we had a gross-income tax with a top rate of 25%, people could hit that top rate and move past it without feeling inordinate pain.

The ideal is hardly ever achieved in real life, however. The gross-income tax sounds fine in theory, but it seems likely that such a tax would quickly be riddled with loopholes and tangled in complexities just like our present income tax. As has been happening with our present law since 1913, special-interest groups would sob to Congress that the tax treated them unfairly, and Congress would pass new laws to take care of the perceived inequities, and then other tearful groups would say those new laws left *them* out in the cold, and in a few years we'd have what we have now: a law hardly anybody can understand.

Another problem of the gross-income tax is that some tough questions of practical politics stand in its way. Our present tax law contains some cozy benefits for the rich, such as the low capital-gains rate, oil-depletion allowances, tax-free interest on certain bonds. The rich are politically powerful. They might well calculate that a gross-income tax would gouge more tax money out of them than the present system. And, in that case, they wouldn't let the present law die without a ferocious fight.

Other kinds of taxes, not based on income, might stand a better chance politically. The gross-income tax could be seen by the rich as simply a reshuffling operation in which their best-loved benefits were taken away. They might swallow a nonincome tax more peacefully, especially if it embodied concepts so new that nobody could accurately predict the effects.

Expenditure tax: This would be a graduated tax on money you spend. The theory is that the amount a family spends is a fair and accurate indication of that family's ability to pay taxes. If a family spends only a few thousand dollars a year, it can be assumed most of the spending is for necessities, and therefore the family should be taxed lightly or not at all. A family that spends $100,000 a year is obviously buying a lot of luxuries and therefore can afford to pay a heavier tax.

Proponents of the expenditure tax say it would improve the nation's economic health because, unlike the income tax, it wouldn't touch any money people managed to save or invest. The expenditure tax would encourage saving and would make it easier for low- and middle-income people to accumulate capital.

In a sense this tax would be something like a national sales tax, but it would be fairer to the lower income strata than an ordinary sales tax because it would be graduated.

Under the state sales taxes we know today, a middle-income man buying a camera or car pays exactly the same tax as a rich man. Under a graduated expenditure tax, the rich man would pay more.

To look at it another way, the expenditure tax might operate something like our present graduated income tax, except that money saved or invested would be deductible. At the end of each year you would declare your income essentially as you do today, but you would be taxed only on the amount that slipped through your fingers. Whatever you saved or invested would be yours to keep, untaxable.

Many noted economists have praised the idea of an expenditure tax. John Stuart Mill, among others, believed strongly that saved money shouldn't be taxed. In the United States two Yale professors of political economy, Irving Fisher and Thomas S. Adams, argued hotly for an expenditure tax throughout the early part of this century and howled in dismay when the nation adopted an income tax in 1913. One of their staunch friends in Congress, Ogden L. Mills, introduced an expenditure-tax bill in 1921. "The income tax is unfair, confusing and contrary to the nation's interests, and will get worse," Mills said prophetically when his bill was defeated.

Opponents of the expenditure tax say its main effect would be to help the rich get richer. If a rich man wanted to, he could spend very little and escape taxes on the great bulk of his income. Mills, Fisher, Adams and other boosters of the tax have always recognized this problem and have suggested various ways around it. One proposal is that, though a man's savings and investments should be sheltered from taxation during his lifetime, his accumulated wealth should be taxed when he dies. Another proposal is that only the first X-thousand of any taxpayer's savings should be sheltered, and he should start paying a graduated tax as soon as he has saved more than that limit.

The expenditure tax sounds fine to me in theory. I morosely suspect, however, that in practice it would be as complicated and confusing as the income tax—and, what's worse, would offer as many chances for cheating and bribery, if not more.

Annual net-wealth tax: Once a year you would be asked to figure out your net worth—the value of all the money, securities and tangible property you own, less the amount of your debts. You would then pay a tax calculated as a percentage of the resulting figure. In most versions of this proposal the tax would be graduated so that the wealthiest citizens paid the biggest percentage.

Proponents of the idea claim it would be simpler than the income tax and would afford less opportunity for cheating. It is hard to keep track of income, they point out, because income is a flow of money rather than a static amount. A revenue agent must study a whole string of transactions—and often a tangled webwork of them—to be sure a taxpayer has stated his year's income honestly. But (theoretically, at least) it would be an easier matter to figure out a man's net wealth as of a certain date. It is easy to look at a man's bank-account records and see how much money the bank was holding for him on December 31, but it is not as easy to go through a whole 12 months of records and figure out how much money flowed through the account during the year.

Boosters of the wealth tax say, indeed, that Congress could make the administration of this tax a charmingly simple matter. All we would need, they say, would be a few new laws. Banks and stockbrokers might be required to send the Revenue Service a copy of each customer's account statement as of December 31. Corporations might send in lists of stockholders and bondholders. There might be a national real-estate registry and a national automobile registry to help IRS find out who owned how much of what.

Cheating would still be perfectly possible, of course. Even the most optimistic wealth-tax advocates admit it. Wealth could be hidden in the form of cash, and rich citizens could stash their money in foreign banks, securities and real estate as easily as they do today. The United States has tax treaties and informal understandings with various foreign nations, under which each nation is supposed to squeal on the others' tax dodgers. In practice, however, nobody goes out of his way to fulfill these treaty obligations. Each nation is absorbed with the problem of catching its own tax cheats and isn't passionately interested in helping other nations catch theirs.

Yet it seems to me that the wealth tax is worth thinking about. Wealth is wealth, no matter what form it takes. Under a wealth tax we probably wouldn't end by trying to treat different types of wealth in different ways, as we do with income. Moreover, a wealth tax would bypass the need to set up a confusing array of deductions against income. We would need no deductions for interest, medical expense, casualty losses and the like. The Revenue Service would need to know one main thing about each taxpayer: how rich he was at the end of the year or on some other established accounting date. Presumably his tax would be affected by a few considerations such as the number of dependents he was trying to support. Beyond that, the tax could be tolerably simple, at least in comparison with the ghastly complexity we're living with now.

Opponents of this tax, particularly those who applaud the expenditure tax, say the wealth tax would discourage saving and hence would be bad for the national economy in the long run. As December 31 approached, people would rush to get rid of taxable wealth. There would be a national buying spree once a year, with the buying concentrated on goods and services that would not show up in the tax rolls as tangible property. The spree would be good for the restaurant and bar business, but not for the automobile business.

How to deal with this problem? One suggestion is that each citizen could be taxed on his gain in body weight during the last month of each year. A more serious suggestion is that the annual tax-accounting day need not be fixed at December 31. The day might be chosen by lottery. The year's 365 dates could be written on slips of paper and dropped in a hat. With appropriate fanfare each December 31, the president or somebody else (a nontaxable hobo might be genially appropriate) could publicly dip his hand into the hat and pull out a day, and that day would be the tax-accounting date for that year.

My own feeling is that this date lottery would bring a little fun into the tax law. Fun is one thing every tax law could use and no tax law has ever had.

The government as holding company: Some people hate taxes so much that they think the federal government should raise revenues without taxation, or with a bare minimum of it. The government could theoretically do this by becoming a major stockholder in industry, or by taking over certain industries and running them as government monopolies. It might take over the airline industry, for example, and earn revenue by charging stiff prices for tickets. Or it might take over the real-estate-brokerage business, or the automobile-manufacturing business.

The trouble with such proposals is that they are nearly unworkable in terms of practical politics. Whenever a taxhater proposes that the government take over a business, the business he has in mind is always somebody else's, not his own. Before the Civil War the U.S. government earned considerable revenue by selling land, but since then nearly all federal money has been raised by tariffs and taxes. The tradition of federal nonparticipation in business goes too deep to be uprooted without a major political upheaval.

It is true that the idea of the government as holding company works well in some countries. Switzerland is an example that brings tears to the eyes of tax-riddled Americans. There is no federal income tax in that utopian land. There are cantonal (state) income taxes, usually with top rates in the range of 25% to 35%. The federal government gets its money through tariffs and sales taxes, and through stock participation in profitable industries such as Swissair. But this setup can work in Switzerland because of a tradition that goes back for centuries. The Swiss are used to seeing government representatives at corporate directors' and stockholders' meetings. As long as the government men keep their mouths shut, which they almost always do, Swiss businessmen accept them as the lesser of two evils—the greater evil being a federal income tax.

There are only a few signs of such a tradition in America. The federal and state governments are in the road-building business, and an occasional government project such as a toll bridge may show a profit. Some state governments run profitable lotteries. The U.S. Post Office earned minor profits back in the dim, dead past. Atomic-energy projects of the future may require government participation, which may produce revenue. But it seems unlikely that business profits will ever add up to a major share of U.S. government revenues, at least in our lifetimes, or that the government will soon abandon its long addiction to taxation.

Value-added tax: This would be a tax paid by businesses, not directly by you and me. But since at least some of the cost would be paid by us as ultimate consumers of what businesses produce, and since the value-added tax has received more than its usual share of publicity in recent years, we might as well look at it briefly.

Essentially, the idea behind it is to tax each producer according to the "value" he adds to a product on its way to the consumer. To oversimplify the idea a bit, let's suppose you've got a little company that earns its living by manufacturing clock springs. You buy your spring steel in bulk. A certain type of spring requires, let's say, 25¢ worth of metal. After you've formed this metal into a spring, you sell it to a clock manufacturer for 75¢. You have therefore added 50¢ to the value of the product, and you pay a tax on that amount. The clock manufacturer, in turn, puts your spring together with other components so as to make an alarm clock, which he sells to a wholesaler for $5.98. Your spring, now embodied in a useful product, is deemed to have increased in value to $1.25, another increment of 50¢. The clockmaker pays a tax on that 50¢ and he is similarly taxed on other components that have increased in value as they passed through his plant. In a sense the value-added tax is something like a universal sales tax.

The French have had a value-added tax since 1948,

and today it brings in about a third of all national revenues in that country. Its proponents say it is better for a nation's economic health than a corporate income tax. The income tax penalizes the most efficient producers, for the more they earn, the more heavily they are taxed. Less efficient producers are taxed more lightly and thus are artificially propped up. The sentimental may say this is a good idea, but the more hardhearted breeds of economists believe in the stern law of natural selection: Only the fittest should survive. The value-added tax would have this unkind effect. Inefficient producers would get little or no tax break and would go out of business faster than they do now, making room for more efficient companies. Presumably, in the long run, this would create a more robust economy.

I'm all in favor of a robust economy. I only wonder how a value-added tax could be administered. It gives me nightmares. It sounds complicated, and it also sounds as though it would be riddled with opportunities to cheat. Even the tax's most ardent advocates admit it might be hard to organize smoothly. Because of this, they often suggest tiptoeing into it as into icy water, rather than plunging up to our necks all at once and perhaps dying of a national thrombosis. There might be a 1% value-added tax to begin with, accompanied by a tiny corresponding drop in income-tax rates. After a couple of years the value-added tax might be raised to 3%, then 7%, and so on, with the income tax gradually withering away simultaneously. The ultimate dream of the value-added-tax folks is, of course, a nation running itself without either corporate or individual income taxes.

I suspect this is only a dream. In the first place, the phase-out period would be absolutely terrifying in its confusion. The Revenue Service can barely administer one major national tax without drowning in paper. How could we handle two? Though income-tax rates would drop as the value-added tax phased in, the number of taxpayers wouldn't drop. We would still have the same number of returns to audit, the same number of cheats to catch, the same number of rules to remember. With the value-added tax added to our problems, IRS might have to double its already huge, unwieldy army of personnel.

In the second place, it is an historical fact that taxes seldom wither away according to the promises of theoreticians and politicians. The value-added tax might be phased in, but it is most unlikely that the income tax would be phased out. An immutable law of government is that you always need more revenue than you thought you were going to need. I can foresee a future year when the value-added tax is up to a top rate of 20% and the income tax is still as high as it always was. "Next year we'll cut the income tax," promises the president. Next year the value-added top rate goes up to 25%. "*Next* year," says the president . . .

National automatic tax: This is more a futuristic dream—a revenue man's flight into science fiction—than a serious proposal. It is sometimes mentioned by computer manufacturers as a feature of their own private and commercial dreams. They predict, or hope for, a world in which all money transactions will flow through computers. Cash will have disappeared in this envisioned world. You will carry some kind of computer-readable card to identify you, or perhaps your thumbprint alone will be enough. Whenever you receive or pay out money, you and the other party to the transaction will accomplish it simply by having your two bank balances adjusted inside some huge, central electronic memory in Washington.

My job will have disappeared by that time—The Internal Revenue Service won't need me; the computer will know precisely how much money you have, where you got it from, how much you spent during the year, where you spent it and what you bought. You won't even need to fill out a tax return. The great central computer will figure out what you owe, and then, silently and inexorably and unemotionally, it will substract the amount from your account balance and shift it to the account of the U.S. Treasury. *Click*—your taxes are paid.

I know this vision is futuristic and perhaps science-fictionish, but I must say it attracts me strongly. It is the only taxation system I can think of which, if set up cleverly, could nearly eliminate cheating.

It would be virtually impossible to hide income if all money transactions were forced to flow through the great central Tax Machine. Every time one man paid money to another man, the machine would know about it, would make a record of it and would consult that record at tax time.

Incurable tax haters could still cheat if they wanted to do so badly enough. An underground flow of illegal cash and illegal IOUs—unofficial checks—would conceivably develop. Suppose Smith owes Jones a thousand bucks. Jones says, "Look, I don't want this transaction to go through the Tax Machine, so I'll make you a deal. You owe me a grand, right? Okay, let's make it just nine hundred. Instead of transacting through the machine, you just give me your personal IOU."

Smith, offered a chance to save $100, thinks this is a nifty idea. Jones goes away with $900 that the Tax Machine will never discover.

At some later date, Jones owes some money to another fellow named Brown. He owes $2,000, let's say. Brown shares Jones's lack of love for the Tax Machine, so he invites Jones to pay with illegal IOUs. Jones endorses Smith's $900 IOU and hands it over, along with his own IOU to make up the balance. In such ways as this a hidden and lawless currency of IOUs could develop.

It is even conceivable that illegal, underground "banks" would develop to serve the IOU trade in much the same way as banks now operate with checks and cash. If you had a bundle of large-denomination IOUs that you wanted to change for smaller denominations, you would have the service performed at a secret bank. The bank would give you a sheaf of $10 and $20 IOUs, extracting a generous fee for the service. The fee might hurt, but it would be smaller than the tax you were evading. If this process went on long enough, IOUs would evolve into a kind of underground cash.

My job, if I were then employed by the Tax Machine Service, would be mainly to stamp out the illegal IOU-cash currency. How big would the job be? Big, I imagine—when cheating is possible, people cheat—but I doubt the total volume of cheating would be anywhere near as big as what we deal with today. It would be inconvenient to transact business in illegal currency, and it could also be made risky. There would have to be an interface between underground and aboveground transactions, and a revenue agent could post himself at this interface and catch evaders sliding from one transaction mode to the other.

There are many who would object to the idea of the Tax Machine because it sounded to them like an encroachment on civil liberties. Nobody's financial affairs would be private anymore. Yet let's remember that people's financial affairs aren't *supposed* to be private today. You are *sup-*

posed to tell IRS everything of substance that there is to know about the flow of money into and out of your pocket. An element of freedom seems to exist because, under our peculiar system of "taxation by confession," widespread cheating is possible. The freedom doesn't exist in the laws; it exists only because nearly everybody breaks the laws.

The laws wouldn't have to be changed if we had a Tax Machine. That machine could operate under any tax law, including the one we know today. The law would grant taxpayers exactly the same degree of freedom that it grants them now. The only difference would be that the Tax Machine wouldn't let them cheat as much.

I've said before that I'm not opposed to cheating in the sense that it offends my feelings about abstract morality. I don't really know what I think about morality. I am not even sure that it is a realistic or useful concept. What troubles me is that our present tax system is unfair to those who for their own reasons don't want to cheat. It is also unfair to those who, though they would love to cheat if they could, are locked into financial situations where the cheating opportunities are restricted. Our system trusts some people's confessions more than others'.

This is why the idea of a Tax Machine attracts me. It is a soundly cynical idea. It does away with the notion of confession, the sentimental and essentially unfair idea of voluntary compliance. It looks the world squarely in the face and sees it for what it is: a tough, competitive world in which people, if they must cheat to survive, cheat.

The Diogenes Machine. It stands there with a lantern, looking for an honest man. It may be a cynical machine, but it is also a profoundly sympathetic one. It knows people are made of flesh and blood.

About the Author

Diogenes is the pseudonym of a tax man who wants his identity protected "until I decide to leave the Internal Revenue Service—which may be quite soon." He adds: "I'm fond of IRS itself. It would be nearly impossible to find a more amiable employer. But I'm not happy with the laws we in IRS must administer, or the ways in which we're sometimes forced to administer them. Since revenue agents are discouraged from expressing judgments about the tax laws in public, and since my book contains such judgments, I must stay hidden if I want to keep my job and go on feeding my family."

Diogenes is in his late thirties. He has a wife and four children, the oldest of whom is a teen-ager "and just had the sobering experience of seeing the first tax bite withheld from his first paycheck." The family lives in a suburban home in what Diogenes calls "a neighborhood of hard-working, IRS-fearing, middle-income taxpayers." He recalls that his neighbors were a little frightened of him when he first moved in years ago, but they accepted him when they realized he was essentially in the same boat. He, like most middle-income Americans, pays more tax than he can really afford.